PALEO COOKING
from Elana's Pantry

PALEO COOKING
from Elana's Pantry

Gluten-Free, Grain-Free, Dairy-Free Recipes

Elana Amsterdam

PHOTOGRAPHY BY LEIGH BEISCH

TEN SPEED PRESS
Berkeley

Contents

Acknowledgments   vi

Introduction   1

The Paleo Pantry ⊚   9

Breakfast ⊚   17

Breads and Crackers ⊚   33

Vegetables ⊚   45

Entrées ⊚   63

Condiments, Spreads, and Toppings ⊚   85

Pies, Pastries, and Crusts ⊚   95

Ice Cream ⊚   103

Cookies and Bars ⊚   111

Beverages ⊚   119

Sources   128

Index   130

Measurement Conversion Charts   137

Acknowledgments

First, thanks to my readers for your support, inspiration, encouragement, and conversation.

Special thanks to my husband—I am truly grateful for your honest feedback regarding my cooking, as well as so many areas of life in general. Thank you for your moral support during all of the deadlines that I faced in creating this book. Thanks also to my two sons J and E for offering highly critical reviews of every dish I make, yet repeatedly doing so in the most loving manner. You are my favorite taste testers.

Many other people supported my vision in a variety of ways that helped to make this book a reality, thus thanks go out to: Sara Golski, Dan Becker, Leigh Beisch, Karin Lazarus, Courtney Behnke, Maggie Locascio, and my wonderful friend Deborah Kinney.

Finally, thanks to Helen McCusker for thirty years of friendship and for overnighting rhubarb to me in Boulder when it was out of season here.

Introduction

I've been eating grain-free for well over a decade, since 2001. While I am very focused on using the foods I eat to improve my health, my primary goal has been to bring people together around *good food*. For me, this means creating tasty dishes that appeal to everyone, not just those with dietary restrictions.

My friends say that when I'm trying to perfect a new recipe I am like a dog with a bone—I don't stop until my recipe tastes like the classic dish that I aim to emulate, sometimes testing a recipe as many as thirty times until I get it just right.

Where does this drive come from? It stems from the love I have for my oldest son (now fourteen, diagnosed with celiac at age two) and my desire for him to have food that is delicious and enticing. In other words, I don't want him to covet the food his friends eat. I want his friends to clamor for the food that I make—and they do. When the boys bring their friends by the house, they all dig in to piles of homemade bagels with healthy spreads, high-protein cookies (made with almond flour), and wholesome ice cream made with coconut milk, hemp seeds, and honey. During sleepovers they raid my kitchen for a midnight snack—little do they know how nutritious the food they are "sneaking" is.

My culinary journey started with an Ayurvedic training that began in 1993. (Ayurveda, or the science of self-healing, is a five-thousand-year-old system that originated in India; it emphasizes balancing the body, mind, and spirit through diet, lifestyle, and exercise.) It became quite handy just a few years later in 1998, when I was diagnosed with celiac disease. Initially, I relied on the gluten-free diet; however, this did little to improve my digestion.

My husband, concerned about my continuing digestive distress, researched solutions and found the Specific Carbohydrate Diet (SCD). This diet was created by the brilliant Elaine Gottschall, with whom I later became friends via a series of long telephone conversations. In 2001 I began eating grain-free, and I have ever since.

In 2006, after several years of creativity in the kitchen, I started my blog, *Elana's Pantry*, where I have a collection of more than seven hundred grain-free recipes.

In the meantime, the grain-free diet, for the most part now referred to as the Paleo (or ancestral) diet, has taken the culinary world by storm. Now, when I'm at book signings, all types of people tell me about their love of Paleo eating; many want to eat like a caveman.

As interest in the Paleo diet has grown, I've adapted many of its additional tenets, including eliminating legumes and dairy. I also avoid some nightshades (including tomatoes, potatoes, peppers, and eggplant), which proponents of the Paleo diet say may possibly be detrimental to those with autoimmune conditions. Further, given the number of friends I have with nut allergies, I've drastically increased the number of nut-free recipes in this book.

As food allergies continue to increase, I am happy to cut out allergens while rising to the challenge of keeping favorite foods flavorfully in the picture. I hope you enjoy this new book and the evolution it has taken from my past work.

WHY PALEO?

For most of humankind's 2.5-million-year existence we have lived as hunter-gatherers. It has only been in the last ten thousand years, with the advent of agriculture, that we have begun to eat the modern grain-based diet.

What we have come to realize, however, is that a grain-based diet may be detrimental to certain individuals. Why? It is possible that not all of us have the genetic makeup to digest grains.

The Paleo diet was first outlined by Dr. S. Boyd Eaton in the *New England Journal of Medicine* in a 1985 article called "Paleolithic Nutrition." It was further researched, refined, and popularized by Dr. Loren Cordain, who writes, "By restoring the food types that we are genetically programmed to eat, we can not only lose weight, but also restore our health and well-being."[1] That's great news for many of us with chronic, untreatable conditions such as multiple sclerosis, diabetes, and arthritis.

Personally, I have found that a plant-based diet with small amounts of lean animal protein makes me feel less inflamed and more energetic. However, for me there is more to a healthy lifestyle than diet. Light exercise and good sleep are also components of our ancestors' lifestyle that we too can employ.

After adopting a grain-free diet, I continued to fine-tune my healing journey by increasing my sleep and reducing the intensity of my exercise. By listening to my body, I figured out that this was what I needed. At that point, I didn't realize that what I was doing was part of a bigger health movement, so I was thrilled when I came across the works of Loren Cordain (*The Paleo Diet*), Robb Wolf (*The Paleo Solution*), and Mark Sisson (*The Primal Blueprint*), as my beliefs and practices closely resembled their own.

1. Cordain, Loren, *The Paleo Diet*. New York: John Wiley & Sons Inc., 2002, 4.

I have benefited so much from implementing my grain-free diet that I decided to write this book to help you get on the road to health as well. If you are already on that road, this book will make your life a little simpler—and tastier, too—with its recipes for quick and healthy dishes made from unprocessed foods.

Eating the way of our ancestors is not a fad. It is a potent solution for people with health conditions, as well as a good strategy for those who are ready to benefit from a healthier diet. Whether you have an autoimmune condition or are a high-performance athlete looking to reduce inflammation and improve your recovery time, the simple, healthy, gluten-free, grain-free, dairy-free, legume-free, and nightshade-free recipes in this book can help you achieve your goals.

With the availability of so many ultramodern foods today, we face many choices. That's why I urge you not only to use these simple, healthy recipes, but also to purchase organic foods whenever possible, eat local and wild foods, and avoid genetically modified products (which, incidentally, are very highly regulated in Europe).

I enjoy eating comforting, familiar dishes that use terrifically healthy ingredients. The dishes on the following pages are those my family and I eat on a daily basis—especially the Roasted Broccoli (page 56) and Avocado Kale Salad (page 46) (which my younger son likes to make for us). I think you'll find that eating a Paleo diet is delicious and, if you choose to make these recipes part of your repertoire, there is really no reason to adhere to the "80-20 rule" advocated by some (eating Paleo foods 80 percent of the time and the standard American diet the remaining 20 percent of the time). As someone with autoimmune conditions, I find that eating gluten- and grain-free foods 100 percent of the time is best for my body, and that the recipes here are satisfying enough to eat day-in and day-out.

PALEO DIET GUIDELINES

People often worry that a grain-free diet does not have enough fiber. However, as you can see from the table below, vegetables and fruit actually have more fiber than grains.

Comparison of Nutritional Values: Grains versus Vegetables and Fruit[2]

Nutrition Info (100 g)	Fiber	Carbohydrates	Protein
Sunflower Seeds (dried)	8.6 g	20.0 g	20.78 g
Avocado (raw)	6.8 g	8.64 g	1.96 g
Broccoli (cooked)	3.3 g	7.18 g	2.38 g
Cabbage (raw)	2.5 g	5.8 g	1.28 g
Potatoes (white, baked)	2.1 g	21.08 g	2.1 g
Brown Rice (long grain, cooked)	1.8 g	22.96 g	2.58 g
White Rice (long grain, cooked)	0.4 g	28.17 g	2.69 g

While it might seem confusing at first to know which foods are or aren't considered Paleo, here are some general guidelines:

Meats. Emphasize lean meat, including cuts of beef, pork, and lamb. Also include poultry such as chicken, turkey, and other types of game. Avoid processed meats such as cold cuts.

Seafood. Seafood, including fish and shellfish, is permitted on the Paleo diet. Eat wild, not farmed, fish, as it is higher in healthy nutrients and not fed pesticides, antibiotics, and dyes. Stick with wild-caught salmon or smaller

2. US Department of Agriculture—Agricultural Research Service, National Nutrient Database, http://ndb.nal.usda.gov/ndb/foods/list.

fish such as flounder, sole, pollock, cod, and halibut. Avoid large fish such as swordfish and tuna, as they tend to accumulate mercury and other toxins.

Vegetables. Green vegetables are a Paleo diet superstar, as they are high in fiber and rich in vitamins, minerals, and important micronutrients. Eat as much kale, broccoli, chard, zucchini, and so on, as you like. Root vegetables such as onions, winter squash, carrots, beets, turnips, and radishes are also excellent foods. Dr. Cordain discourages the consumption of white potatoes, and I personally adhere to this recommendation.

Fruit. Fruit is a wonderful source of fiber (which slows down the absorption of the accompanying sugar), antioxidants, and phytochemicals. Include fruit such as apples, apricots, avocados, bananas, all types of berries, figs, kiwis, mangoes, melons, and citrus, including lemons, limes, and oranges. If you are trying to lose weight, limit your fruit intake. Because dried fruit and juice have a high glycemic load, Cordain recommends that these foods are eaten in minimal quantities by everyone.

Nuts and Seeds. Nuts and seeds are rich in fat and fiber and full of good protein. Cordain recommends limiting consumption to less than four ounces per day for those trying to lose weight, however, because of a high level of omega-6 fats (which in excess can cause inflammation) I recommend that those following a Paleo diet consume no more than an ounce per day, which is about a handful. This is why so many of the baked goods recipes in this book are made with coconut flour rather than nut flour. Just a note, peanuts are not permitted on the Paleo diet, as they are a legume, not a nut.

Fats and Oils. Coconut oil, palm oil, cocoa butter, and lard are permitted on the Paleo diet for cooking and other uses. Cordain states that olive oil is a good oil, though not a "best" oil and is to be used for cooking less than the aforementioned oils.

Eggs. Cordain states that our ancestors only had access to eggs on a seasonal basis and that it is best to keep egg consumption to around six per week. Personally, I tend to eat just a bit more than that. I buy chicken eggs that are high in omega-3 fatty acids, as they are nutritionally superior to the eggs of chickens fed a diet high in omega-6 grains.

Foods to Avoid. The Paleo diet does not include the consumption of cereal grains, dairy, or legumes (a fancy name for beans), therefore the recipes in this book are grain-free, gluten-free, dairy-free, and legume-free. The Paleo diet also does not include the consumption of processed foods such as soft drinks and candy.

Exceptions. I make an exception (as many Paleo cookbook authors do) when it comes to a few select foods by including small amounts of salt, some modern condiments (such as oil, vinegar, and mustard), and the ingredients to make some treats (baking soda, vanilla extract, honey, stevia, and chocolate). If you are trying to eat exactly like a caveman, don't use those foods. And don't cook on a stove. And don't . . . well, you get the idea. For me the Paleo diet is about eating healthy, and at the same time, not feeling deprived. As always, modify and adapt to what works best for you.

HOW TO USE THIS BOOK

I have included a sweetness indicator for many of these recipes. It will let you know which dishes to make when you are in the mood for a slightly sweet treat or a more decadent dessert. Recipes that do not have a significant amount of sweetener do not have a sweetness indicator.

Many of the recipes in this book are allergen-free. The following symbols indicate which recipes are suitable for nut-free and vegan diets.

Nut-free: Ⓜ   Vegan: Ⓥ

The Paleo Pantry

The recipes in this book are made of real food, the kind that grows in your garden, can be hunted in a field, or caught from a stream. These recipes are also simple, because as much as I love to cook, I have plenty of other priorities that take place outside of the kitchen.

A couple of things are important when making the recipes in this book. First, use the precise ingredients specified here (see the description of ingredients that follows). Second, note that because many of the ingredients used here are so new on the market, they often vary a great deal from brand to brand, so please use the brands listed.

Finally, in the words of the great Ina Garten, "Follow the recipe precisely when you make it the first time. After that, you can always modify it to your personal taste." This is even more important when it comes to using new ingredients that are less familiar to you. So follow each recipe to a "T" the first time you make it, then experiment on your second or third time around.

The following are some of the ingredients and equipment I use in this book. For information on where to purchase these items, please refer to the Sources section on page 128.

ALMOND FLOUR

I have written an entire book on almond flour, and it's one of my favorite ingredients. Made from blanched and very finely ground almonds, this ingredient is rich in flavor, easy to use, and very healthy. I highly recommend Honeyville almond flour for these recipes—it is what I use in my own kitchen.

ARROWROOT POWDER

I use arrowroot powder as a thickener in syrups and sauces instead of cornstarch, as many people (including myself) cannot tolerate corn and its by-products.

CHIA SEEDS

Chia seeds are highly nutritious and one of the only vegetarian sources of omega-3 fatty acids. I use ground chia seeds in Hot Cereal (page 28). For more chia seed recipes, go to my blog, *Elana's Pantry*.

CHOCOLATE

I use Dagoba dark chocolate chips that are 73 percent cacao. I have also experimented with a fabulous new brand called Kallari and had excellent results with their chocolate as well.

COCONUT CREAM CONCENTRATE

I discovered coconut cream concentrate a few years ago, and I've recently begun using it in a number of my recipes. Often referred to as coconut butter, it is simply coconut meat in a concentrated form.

COCONUT FLOUR

Coconut flour is made from finely ground, dried, and defatted coconut. It is high in fiber and low in carbohydrates.

Coconut flour is fabulous for baking and results in light and fluffy muffins and cakes. It is unique in that a little goes a very long way. Recipes that use coconut flour use an extremely high ratio of wet ingredients to dry that is very different from the ratios used in typical baking. This is because coconut flour sucks up a ton of moisture. Everything I know about coconut flour I learned from Bruce Fife's fantastic book *Cooking with Coconut Flour*.

COCONUT MILK

Creating a cookbook with everything from dinners to sauces to desserts without using dairy is not a simple feat. Coconut milk makes this challenge possible, and tasty to boot.

For recipes such as Coconut Whipped Cream (page 93) and Basil Cream Sauce (page 86), I use the fat from a can of coconut milk. I have a trick (which I learned from Marla, who blogs about healthy food at *Family Fresh Cooking*) for getting the fat out of the can easily. First, place a can of coconut milk in your refrigerator overnight. Take it out of the refrigerator and place it on your counter upside down. Remove the lid (actually, the bottom) from the can and pour out the liquid, which you can reserve for smoothies or another use. You will be left with the coconut fat. Be sure to purchase regular coconut milk; do not buy reduced-fat or "lite" versions for any of the recipes in this book, as they will not work.

COCONUT OIL

I recommend using unrefined virgin coconut oil in many of my recipes. Store it at room temperature, and melt it over very low heat prior to use. I use coconut oil for sautéing vegetables, as an ingredient in baked goods, and in smoothies.

Even though it was once strongly frowned upon, coconut oil is now rapidly gaining favor among the traditional medical establishment. Allopathic doctors are citing its positive effects on HDL cholesterol and triglycerides, as well as its potentially neuro-protective properties. Personally, I just like the way it tastes.

COCONUT PALM SUGAR

I use organic blonde coconut palm sugar from Sweet Tree for recipes such as Blueberry Coffee Cake (page 24) and Banana Bread (page 40), among others. Coconut sugar has a lovely caramel flavor that is somewhat similar to that of brown sugar. This sweetener is low on the glycemic index. However, given that all sweeteners, from honey to fruit juice concentrate, are best consumed in small amounts, I use it and all other sweeteners in this book sparingly, reserving them for special occasion treats.

EGG WHITE PROTEIN POWDER

Several years ago my dear friend Betsy introduced me to Frank Zane protein powder. Healthy and delicious, it contains pure egg white protein along with stevia. I use this ingredient in smoothies, and I've been experimenting with putting it in various protein bar recipes that I'm developing for my blog.

FLAX MEAL

Flax meal is made by grinding whole flaxseeds. It is best to store this ingredient in the freezer, as it is full of powerful oils and compounds that can go rancid very quickly. I use both golden and brown flax meal, depending on the results that I want. In my recipe for Bagels (page 19), I use golden flax meal, as it makes the bagels light and airy and gives them a nice lift. I use brown flax meal in my Nut-Free Bran Muffins (page 21), as it imparts a heartier taste and deeper, darker color.

HEMP

I use hemp seeds in my recipe for Nut-Free Crackers (page 42) and in many of my ice creams. I learned about using hemp seeds in ice cream from my friend Kelly Brozyna at the Spunky Coconut website. Kelly wrote the book on dairy-free ice cream called *The Spunky Coconut Dairy-Free Ice Cream*.

HONEY

I use wildflower honey from Madhava, which I purchase in a glass jar. I don't like buying ingredients in plastic containers due to the endocrine-disrupting chemicals that plastic can contain, as well as the odd flavor that it sometimes imparts.

MUSTARD

Mustard lends a delicious flavor to dressings, poultry, and fish. Be sure to purchase a brand of Dijon mustard that does not contain added sugar. I recommend True Natural Taste Certified Organic Stone Ground Dijon Mustard, which I purchase at my local Whole Foods.

NUT AND SEED BUTTERS

I use a variety of nut and seed butters in my recipes, including almond butter, macadamia nut butter, and sunflower seed butter. Nut and seed butters are high-protein, nutritionally dense foods that add delicious flavor and texture to everything from sauces to ice creams. While most home cooks are familiar with almond butter and macadamia nut butter, sunflower seed butter is a nut-free alternative that is a fabulous replacement for peanut butter and other nut butters.

OLIVE OIL

I use a high-quality extra-virgin olive oil for dressing salads and most other cooking projects. Be sure to use a very mild-flavored olive oil when making Paleo Mayonnaise (page 88).

SALT

Stick with Celtic sea salt in these recipes, as it tastes a tad less salty than other types. I use finely ground Celtic sea salt in my recipes because you don't want to end up with little boulders of salt in your baked goods.

SESAME OIL

I love the flavor of sesame oil, which adds an Asian flair to many of my entrée and vegetable recipes. Use Eden Select brand *toasted* sesame oil for the best results. Raw sesame oil does not impart the delicious nutty flavor that the toasted version contains.

SHORTENING

I use Spectrum all-vegetable shortening, made of organic palm oil, in everything from Paleo Pancakes (page 22) to Blueberry Coffee Cake (page 24). While I like to use coconut oil in many of my recipes, I choose shortening when I want to create a more traditional and neutral flavor profile.

SPICE HUNTER SEASONINGS

Spice Hunter seasoning blends, which are gluten-free and made from fresh spices, are a convenient shortcut when you want to add lots of flavor to recipes without using a laundry list of spices. I use their Greek Seasoning in the Greek Turkey Burgers (page 77). I purchase my Spice Hunter seasonings online—they have an incredible selection of high-quality blends.

STEVIA

Stevia is a wonderful herbal sweetener made from the stevia plant. I use stevia in the liquid form, as it has fewer additives than the powdered type. The key to choosing stevia is to pick a brand that does not have a strong aftertaste. I use SweetLeaf brand stevia (liquid) in both the plain and vanilla crème flavors.

UME PLUM VINEGAR

I was introduced to ume plum vinegar during my Ayurvedic training. This vinegar, made from umeboshi plums, has a lovely tart taste and adds incredible flavor to savory dishes. Use Eden Select brand ume plum vinegar.

VANILLA EXTRACT

Please don't skimp on vanilla! Using a high-quality vanilla extract will make all the difference in your recipes. I use organic gluten-free vanilla extract manufactured by Flavorganics.

FOOD PROCESSOR

I use my food processor almost every day to make everything from burgers to baked goods. It is one of my favorite kitchen tools.

HIGH-POWERED BLENDER

The Vitamix is the most used appliance in my kitchen. I use it for ice cream, sauces, smoothies, and shakes.

MAGIC LINE LOAF PAN

After testing my bread recipes in pans of many different sizes and types, I've found that the 7.5 by 3.5-inch Magic Line loaf pan is perfect. In my tests, standard-size loaf pans were too big and left the bread under-cooked, but this pan does the trick, turning out gorgeous loaves. Use it for Paleo Bread (page 34), Nut-Free Bread (page 36), Rye Bread (page 37), and Banana Bread (page 40).

Breakfast

Bagels ◉ 19

Apricot Muffins ◉ 20

Nut-Free Bran Muffins ◉ 21

Paleo Pancakes ◉ 22

Crepes ◉ 23

Blueberry Coffee Cake ◉ 24

Cinnamon French Toast ◉ 26

Cran-Apple Power Bars ◉ 27

Hot Cereal ◉ 28

Super Spice Granola ◉ 29

Breakfast Sausage ◉ 31

Strawberry Power Piña Colada ◉ 32

Bagels

I hadn't had a bagel in more than a decade when Jenni Hulet, author of the blog *The Urban Poser*, left a comment on my website alerting me that she had made grain-free bagels. I serve these toasted and topped with smoked salmon and scrambled eggs.

$1^1/_2$ cups blanched almond flour
$^1/_4$ cup golden flax meal
1 tablespoon coconut flour
1 teaspoon baking soda
$^1/_4$ teaspoon sea salt
5 large eggs
2 tablespoons apple cider vinegar
1 tablespoon poppy seeds (optional)

Preheat the oven to 350°F. Grease a donut pan with coconut oil and dust with coconut flour.

In a food processor, pulse together the almond flour, flax meal, coconut flour, baking soda, and salt. Add the eggs and vinegar and pulse until thoroughly combined.

Place the batter in a resealable plastic bag, snip off one corner, and pipe the batter into the prepared pan. Sprinkle the bagels with poppy seeds.

Bake for 20 to 25 minutes, until a knife inserted into the center of a bagel comes out clean. Let the bagels cool in the pan for 1 hour, then serve.

To store, leave at room temperature overnight, then refrigerate in an airtight container.

Apricot Muffins

MAKES 8 MUFFINS ● SWEETNESS: MEDIUM ● Ⓜ

Delicately flavored, these apricot muffins are a great way to start your day along with a cup of Dandelion Root Coffee (page 121). Or, topped with a little frosting, they're a wonderfully healthy dessert.

$1/_2$ cup dried apricots

$1/_4$ cup coconut flour

$1/_4$ teaspoon baking soda

$1/_4$ teaspoon sea salt

4 large eggs

$1/_2$ cup coconut oil, melted over very low heat

$1/_8$ teaspoon vanilla crème stevia

Preheat the oven to 350°F. Line 8 muffin cups with paper liners.

In a food processor, pulse the apricots for 1 to 2 minutes until well chopped into small pieces; they may form a ball. Pulse in the coconut flour, baking soda, and salt, then pulse in the eggs, coconut oil, and stevia until thoroughly combined.

Scoop $1/_4$ cup of the batter into each prepared muffin cup.

Bake for 15 to 25 minutes, until a toothpick inserted into the center of a muffin comes out with just a few moist crumbs attached. Let the muffins cool in the pan for 1 hour, then serve.

Nut-Free Bran Muffins

MAKES 8 MUFFINS ◉ SWEETNESS: LOW ◉ Ⓜ

I love the healthy taste of a satisfying bran muffin. Pack a couple for an early morning hike, or serve these at brunch alongside scrambled eggs.

½ cup brown flax meal
¼ cup pumpkin seeds
1 tablespoon coconut flour
¼ teaspoon baking soda
¼ teaspoon sea salt
½ cup Medjool dates, pitted
3 large eggs
2 tablespoons coconut oil, melted over very low heat
½ cup raisins
¼ cup sesame seeds
¼ cup sunflower seeds

Preheat the oven to 350°F. Line 8 muffin cups with paper liners.

In a food processor, pulse together the flax meal, pumpkin seeds, coconut flour, baking soda, and salt until the mixture is the texture of sand. Add the dates and pulse for 60 seconds, or until the dates are well chopped. Pulse in the eggs and coconut oil until thoroughly combined. Remove the blade from the food processor and stir in the raisins, sesame seeds, and sunflower seeds.

Scoop ¼ cup of the batter into each prepared muffin cup.

Bake for 20 to 25 minutes, or until a toothpick inserted into the center of a muffin comes out with just a few moist crumbs attached. Let the muffins cool in the pan for 1 hour, then serve.

Paleo Pancakes

MAKES 18 PANCAKES ◉ SWEETNESS: LOW

Serve these fluffy silver dollar–sized pancakes with Strawberry Applesauce (page 94) for a spectacularly flavorful yet healthy breakfast.

1 cup blanched almond flour

¼ cup golden flax meal

2 tablespoons coconut flour

½ teaspoon baking soda

¼ teaspoon sea salt

5 large eggs

¼ cup Spectrum all-vegetable shortening

1 tablespoon honey

1 tablespoon apple cider vinegar

2 tablespoons coconut oil

In a food processor, pulse together the almond flour, flax meal, coconut flour, baking soda, and salt. Add the eggs, shortening, honey, and vinegar and pulse until thoroughly combined.

Heat 2 teaspoons of the coconut oil in a large skillet over medium heat. Scoop 1 heaping tablespoon of the batter onto the skillet for each pancake. Cook until small bubbles begin to form on the top of each pancake. When the bubbles burst, flip the pancakes and cook until lightly browned on the second side, then transfer the pancakes to a plate.

Repeat the process with the remaining oil and batter, then serve.

Crepes

MAKES 6 CREPES ⊙ ⓜ

Simple crepes turn into a decadent, healthy breakfast when filled with homemade Cherry Berry Syrup (page 92) and smothered in Coconut Whipped Cream (page 93). The batter will look watery, but don't worry; it will thicken up nicely when cooked.

2 tablespoons coconut flour
4 large eggs
1 tablespoon coconut oil, melted over very low heat
$1/2$ cup water
2 tablespoons coconut oil

In a food processor, pulse together the coconut flour and eggs. Add the coconut oil and water and pulse until thoroughly combined.

Heat 1 teaspoon of the coconut oil in an 8-inch skillet over medium-low heat. Scoop $1/4$ cup of the batter onto the skillet, tilting the skillet to spread the batter to the edges of the pan. Cook until small bubbles form and burst on the surface of the crepe, then flip and cook the other side, 4 to 5 minutes total. Transfer the crepe to a plate.

Repeat the process with the remaining oil and batter, then serve.

Blueberry Coffee Cake

SERVES 8 ● SWEETNESS: MEDIUM

Slices of this blueberry coffee cake, which show off vibrant splashes of blue, will impress your guests at brunch. It also makes a lovely dessert.

Cake
2 cups blanched almond flour
$1/4$ teaspoon baking soda
$1/4$ teaspoon sea salt
4 large eggs
$1/4$ cup Spectrum all-vegetable shortening
$1/4$ cup coconut sugar
1 tablespoon vanilla extract
$1/2$ cup frozen blueberries

Topping
$1/4$ cup Spectrum all-vegetable shortening
$1/4$ cup coconut sugar
$1/2$ cup blanched almond flour
1 tablespoon ground cinnamon

Preheat the oven to 350°F. Grease an 8-inch round cake pan with shortening and dust with almond flour.

To make the cake, combine the almond flour, baking soda, and salt in a large bowl. In a medium bowl, whisk together the eggs, shortening, coconut sugar, and vanilla extract. Stir the wet ingredients into the almond flour mixture until thoroughly combined, then stir in the blueberries. Pour the batter into the prepared cake pan.

To make the topping, cream together the shortening and coconut sugar in a medium bowl. Stir in the almond flour and cinnamon, then sprinkle the topping over the cake batter.

Bake for 30 to 40 minutes, until a toothpick inserted into the center of the cake comes out with just a few moist crumbs attached. Let the cake cool in the pan for 1 hour, then serve.

Cinnamon French Toast

MAKES 8 SLICES ● SWEETNESS: LOW

French toast topped with Strawberry Applesauce (page 94) and sprinkled with cinnamon? Yes, please!

4 large eggs
¼ cup coconut milk
1 tablespoon honey
1 tablespoon vanilla extract
1 teaspoon ground cinnamon
¼ teaspoon sea salt
8 (½-inch-thick) slices Paleo Bread (page 34)
2 tablespoons coconut oil

In a medium bowl, whisk together the eggs, coconut milk, honey, vanilla extract, cinnamon, and salt until thoroughly combined. Pour the mixture into a 13 by 9-inch baking dish and add the slices of bread. Let the bread soak in the egg mixture for 5 minutes, then turn the slices and soak for 5 more minutes.

Heat 1 tablespoon of the coconut oil in a large skillet over medium-high heat. Add 4 slices of the bread to the skillet and cook for 3 to 5 minutes per side, until well browned on both sides, turning once. When done, transfer the French toast to a plate.

Repeat the process with the remaining oil and bread, then serve.

Cran-Apple Power Bars

MAKES 12 BARS ● SWEETNESS: MEDIUM

My younger son does not care for chocolate. So when he asked for an energy bar that was made with apples, I couldn't refuse. Pack one of these along with your lunch or enjoy it as an on-the-go breakfast on busy mornings.

1¼ cups walnuts, lightly toasted

1 cup unsweetened dried apples

½ cup fruit juice–sweetened dried cranberries

¼ cup egg white protein powder

3 tablespoons water

In a food processor, pulse the walnuts until they are the texture of coarse gravel. Add the apples, cranberries, protein powder, and water and pulse until thoroughly combined.

Press the mixture into an 8-inch square baking dish and refrigerate for at least 1 hour.

Cut into 12 squares and serve. Store in a covered container in the refrigerator.

Hot Cereal

SERVES 2 ⊙ Ⓥ

Growing up, I loved eating Cream of Wheat for breakfast, because there's nothing like starting your day with hot cereal. Now I have this hearty Paleo version. On weekdays I keep it simple; on weekends, I dress it up with Almond Milk (page 127), currants, baked apples, or shredded coconut.

1/3 cup walnuts

1/4 cup unsweetened shredded coconut

1/4 cup golden flax meal

1 tablespoon ground chia seeds

1 tablespoon ground cinnamon

1/4 teaspoon sea salt

2 cups boiling water

In a high-powered blender, grind the walnuts, shredded coconut, flax meal, and chia seeds until smooth. Blend in the cinnamon and salt until thoroughly combined. Pour the boiling water into the blender and cover with the lid. Blend very carefully, starting on the lowest setting, then moving to high, until the mixture is smooth.

Transfer the mixture to a saucepan and cook over low heat for 10 minutes, stirring occasionally (cooking makes the cereal easier to digest). Divide the cereal between 2 bowls and serve.

Super Spice Granola

SERVES 8 ◉ SWEETNESS: MEDIUM ◉ Ⓥ

Crunchy granola, full of antioxidant-rich spices, makes an ideal breakfast served with Almond Milk (page 127). If your oven doesn't go as low as 135°F, set it to 250°F and bake the granola for 90 minutes, or until it's golden brown, then let it cool and dry for an hour before eating. If you are lucky enough to have a dehydrator, experiment with making it in that.

2 quarts plus $1/2$ cup water
2 cups walnuts
1 cup macadamia nuts
1 cup pumpkin seeds
1 cup raisins
1 tablespoon ground cinnamon
$1/2$ teaspoon ground ginger
$1/4$ teaspoon ground cardamom
$1/4$ teaspoon sea salt

In a large bowl, combine 2 quarts of the water, walnuts, macadamia nuts, and pumpkin seeds and let soak overnight. In a separate bowl, soak the raisins in the remaining $1/2$ cup of water overnight.

Preheat the oven to 135°F. Line 2 large baking sheets with parchment paper.

In a food processor, pulse the raisins and their soaking water until smooth. Add the cinnamon, ginger, cardamom, and salt and pulse until thoroughly combined.

In a fine-mesh strainer, drain and rinse the nut mixture. Discard the soaking water. Add the nut mixture to the raisin puree and pulse until the mixture is the consistency of granola.

Transfer the mixture to the prepared baking sheets. Bake for 24 hours, then remove from the oven and let cool. Break into pieces and serve.

Store in a glass jar in the refrigerator for up to 1 week.

Breakfast Sausage

MAKES 8 PATTIES ⊙ Ⓜ

I've modified Alton Brown's recipe for classic breakfast sausage by increasing the sage and removing the refined sugar. For sausage with a milder flavor, reduce the amount of sage to 1 tablespoon. These sausages are perfect served with the Green Frittata (page 80) and Salsa Verde (page 89).

1$^1/_2$ pounds organic ground pork or turkey
2 tablespoons minced fresh sage
1 tablespoon minced fresh rosemary
1 tablespoon honey
1$^1/_2$ teaspoons sea salt
1 teaspoon freshly ground black pepper
1 tablespoon olive oil

In a large bowl, combine the ground pork, sage, rosemary, honey, salt, and pepper, using your hands to mix the ingredients thoroughly.

Using a $^1/_3$-cup measuring cup, form the mixture into 8 patties, each about 2$^1/_4$ inches in diameter.

Heat the olive oil in a large skillet over medium-low heat. Cook the patties, turning them once and gently pressing them down to flatten, for 5 to 8 minutes per side, until golden brown and crispy. Transfer the patties to a paper towel–lined plate and serve.

< Breakfast Sausage with Green Frittata (page 80) and Salsa Verde (page 89)

Strawberry Power Piña Colada

SERVES 2 ◉ SWEETNESS: MEDIUM ◉ Ⓜ

Why add coconut oil to a smoothie? First, it imparts a rich, creamy texture; second, it has potentially neuro-protective properties. I try to eat a tablespoon of coconut oil each day.

³/₄ cup bottled coconut water
¹/₂ cup coconut milk
1 cup frozen pineapple chunks
1 cup frozen strawberries
1 tablespoon coconut oil, at room temperature
¹/₄ cup egg white protein powder

In a high-powered blender, puree the coconut water, coconut milk, pineapple, and strawberries until smooth. Blend in the coconut oil and protein powder until thoroughly combined, then serve.

Breads and Crackers

Paleo Bread ☉ 34

Nut-Free Bread ☉ 36

Rye Bread ☉ 37

Date Orange Bread ☉ 39

Banana Bread ☉ 40

Paleo Tortillas ☉ 41

Nut-Free Crackers ☉ 42

Garlic Crackers ☉ 43

Olive Oil Thyme Crackers ☉ 44

Paleo Bread

MAKES 1 LOAF (ABOUT 12 SLICES)

A little gem of grain-free deliciousness, Paleo Bread works well with both savory and sweet toppings. Try it with Salmon Salad (page 73) or homemade jam.

2 cups blanched almond flour
$\frac{1}{4}$ cup golden flax meal
2 tablespoons coconut flour
$\frac{1}{2}$ teaspoon baking soda
$\frac{1}{4}$ teaspoon sea salt
5 large eggs
1 tablespoon coconut oil, melted over very low heat
1 tablespoon honey
1 tablespoon apple cider vinegar

Preheat the oven to 350°F. Grease a 7 by 3-inch loaf pan with coconut oil.

In a food processor, pulse together the almond flour, flax meal, coconut flour, baking soda, and salt. Add the eggs, coconut oil, honey, and vinegar and pulse until thoroughly combined.

Scoop the batter into the prepared loaf pan and bake for 35 to 45 minutes, until a knife inserted into the center of the loaf comes out clean. Let the bread cool in the pan for 1 hour, then serve.

Nut-Free Bread

MAKES 1 LOAF (ABOUT 12 SLICES) ⊙ Ⓜ

There's nothing like sitting in your kitchen with friends eating toasted bread alongside a warm bowl of Healing Vegetable Bisque (page 55). I created this recipe for those with both nut and gluten allergies.

$^3/_4$ cup coconut flour

1 teaspoon baking soda

$^1/_2$ teaspoon sea salt

4 large eggs

$^1/_2$ cup olive oil

2 tablespoons honey

$^1/_4$ cup golden flax meal, soaked in $^1/_2$ cup water for 10 minutes

Preheat the oven to 350°F. Grease a 7 by 3-inch loaf pan with olive oil.

In a food processor, pulse together the coconut flour, baking soda, and salt. Add the eggs, olive oil, and honey and pulse until thoroughly combined, then pulse in the flax meal–water mixture.

Scoop the batter into the prepared loaf pan and bake for 35 to 45 minutes, until a knife inserted into the center of the loaf comes out clean. Let the bread cool in the pan for 1 hour, then serve.

Rye Bread

MAKES 1 LOAF (ABOUT 12 SLICES)

Before I was diagnosed with celiac disease I loved the savory perfume of a good rye bread. Since rye has gluten in it, that's not an option for me anymore, but the piquant caraway seeds in this bread give it a similar hearty flavor.

1 cup blanched almond flour
3/4 cup brown flax meal
1/2 teaspoon baking soda
1/2 teaspoon sea salt
4 large eggs
1 tablespoon olive oil
2 tablespoons caraway seeds

Preheat the oven to 350°F. Grease a 7 by 3-inch loaf pan with olive oil.

In a large bowl, combine the almond flour, flax meal, baking soda, and salt. In a medium bowl, whisk together the eggs and olive oil. Stir the wet ingredients into the almond flour mixture until thoroughly combined, then stir in the caraway seeds.

Scoop the batter into the prepared loaf pan and bake for 30 to 40 minutes, until a knife inserted into the center of the loaf comes out clean. Let the bread cool in the pan for 1 hour, then serve.

Date Orange Bread

MAKES 1 SMALL LOAF (ABOUT 8 SLICES) ⊙ SWEETNESS: MEDIUM ⊙ Ⓜ

Thinking of your neighbors during the holidays? Give them date orange loaves wrapped in parchment and tied with festive ribbon. They'll never guess it's gluten-free!

$1/3$ cup coconut flour

1 teaspoon baking soda

$1/4$ teaspoon sea salt

4 large eggs

$1/2$ cup coconut oil, melted over very low heat

1 tablespoon firmly packed orange zest

$1/2$ cup Medjool dates, pitted and chopped

Preheat the oven to 350°F. Grease a 5 by 3-inch mini loaf pan with coconut oil.

In a food processor, pulse together the coconut flour, baking soda, and salt. Add the eggs, coconut oil, and orange zest and pulse until thoroughly combined. Remove the blade from the food processor and stir in the dates.

Scoop the batter into the prepared loaf pan and bake for 25 to 35 minutes, until a knife inserted into the center of the loaf comes out with just a few moist crumbs attached. Let the bread cool in the pan for 1 hour, then serve.

Banana Bread

MAKES 1 LOAF (ABOUT 12 SLICES) ⊙ SWEETNESS: MEDIUM

Turn those old bananas that your children won't touch into an enticingly rich banana bread made with coconut oil, coconut sugar, and coconut flour.

1 cup blanched almond flour
1 tablespoon coconut flour
$1/4$ teaspoon baking soda
$1/4$ teaspoon sea salt
4 large eggs
2 tablespoons coconut oil, melted over very low heat
2 tablespoons coconut sugar
2 to 3 very ripe bananas, mashed (about 1 cup)

Preheat the oven to 350°F. Grease a 7 by 3-inch loaf pan with coconut oil and dust with almond flour.

In a large bowl, combine the almond flour, coconut flour, baking soda, and salt. In a medium bowl, whisk together the eggs, coconut oil, and coconut sugar until thoroughly combined, then stir in the bananas. Stir the wet ingredients into the almond flour mixture until thoroughly combined.

Scoop the batter into the prepared loaf pan and bake for 50 to 60 minutes, until a knife inserted into the center of the loaf comes out with just a few moist crumbs attached. Let the bread cool in the pan for 1 hour, then serve.

Paleo Tortillas

MAKES 4 TORTILLAS ◉ Ⓜ

I based this recipe on one from Mark's Daily Apple, a favorite website of mine. Serve with Rosemary Lemon Chicken (page 70), shredded lettuce, and sliced avocados for a simple south-of-the-border meal. My neighbor Josh can eat an entire batch of these at a time and says they are even better than regular tortillas.

1 tablespoon coconut flour
1/8 teaspoon baking soda
3 large eggs
1 tablespoon plus 4 teaspoons olive oil
1 tablespoon freshly squeezed lime juice
1/3 cup water

In a food processor, pulse together the coconut flour and baking soda. Add the eggs, 1 tablespoon of the olive oil, lime juice, and water and pulse until thoroughly combined. Let the batter stand for 20 minutes to thicken.

Heat 1 teaspoon of the olive oil in an 8-inch skillet over medium-low heat. Scoop 1/4 cup of the batter onto the skillet, tilting the skillet to spread the batter to the edges of the pan. Cook until small bubbles form and burst, then flip the tortilla and cook until the second side is lightly browned. Transfer the tortilla to a plate.

Repeat the process with the remaining oil and batter, then serve.

Nut-Free Crackers

MAKES 16 CRACKERS ⊙ Ⓜ Ⓥ

Finally! Hearty crackers that are gluten-free, grain-free, egg-free, nut-free—and mighty tasty too. Serve these with the Easy Avocado Dip from my blog *Elana's Pantry*.

$1/3$ cup hemp seeds
$1/3$ cup sesame seeds
1 tablespoon coconut flour
$1/3$ cup golden flax meal
$1/2$ teaspoon sea salt
1 tablespoon Spectrum all-vegetable shortening
2 tablespoons water

Preheat the oven to 350°F. Set aside 2 large baking sheets. Cut 3 pieces of parchment paper to the size of the baking sheets.

In a food processor, pulse together the hemp seeds and sesame seeds until the mixture is the texture of coarse gravel. Pulse in the coconut flour, flax meal, and salt, then pulse in the shortening and water until the dough forms a ball.

Divide the dough into 2 equal pieces. Place 1 piece of dough between 2 sheets of parchment paper and roll into a rectangle about 4 inches by 8 inches and $1/8$ inch thick. Remove the top piece of parchment paper and transfer the bottom piece of parchment paper with the rolled-out dough onto a baking sheet. Repeat the process with the remaining piece of dough. Cut the dough into 2-inch squares with a knife or pizza cutter.

Bake the crackers for 10 to 15 minutes, until golden brown. Let the crackers cool on the baking sheets for 30 minutes, then serve.

Garlic Crackers

MAKES 24 CRACKERS

Robustly flavored garlic crackers are healthier than potato chips and taste every bit as good. Snack on them plain or top with your favorite dip.

$1^1/_2$ cups blanched almond flour
$^1/_4$ teaspoon sea salt
$^1/_8$ teaspoon baking soda
1 large egg
1 tablespoon minced fresh garlic

Preheat the oven to 350°F. Set aside 2 large baking sheets. Cut 3 pieces of parchment paper to the size of the baking sheets.

In a food processor, pulse together the almond flour, salt, and baking soda. Add the egg and garlic and pulse until thoroughly combined.

Divide the dough into 2 equal pieces. Place 1 piece of dough between 2 sheets of parchment paper and roll into a rectangle about 6 inches by 8 inches and $^1/_{16}$ inch thick. Remove the top piece of parchment paper and transfer the bottom piece of parchment with the rolled-out dough onto a baking sheet. Repeat the process with the remaining piece of dough. Cut the dough into 2-inch squares with a knife or pizza cutter.

Bake the crackers for 8 to 10 minutes, until golden brown. Let the crackers cool on the baking sheets for 30 minutes, then serve.

Olive Oil Thyme Crackers

MAKES 24 CRACKERS ◉ Ⓥ

Vegan crackers flavored with superfood thyme and packed with highly nutritious almond flour are a family favorite. Serve these with olive tapenade; you can find the recipe for this and other spreads on my blog.

$1^3/_4$ cups blanched almond flour
1 tablespoon minced fresh thyme
$^1/_2$ teaspoon sea salt
1 tablespoon olive oil
2 tablespoons water

Preheat the oven to 350°F. Set aside 2 large baking sheets. Cut 3 pieces of parchment paper to the size of the baking sheets.

In a food processor, pulse together the almond flour, thyme, and salt. Add the olive oil and water and pulse until thoroughly combined.

Divide the dough into 2 equal pieces. Place 1 piece of dough between 2 sheets of parchment paper and roll into a rectangle about 6 inches by 8 inches and $^1/_{16}$ inch thick. Remove the top piece of parchment paper and transfer the bottom piece of parchment with the rolled-out dough onto a baking sheet. Repeat the process with the remaining piece of dough. Cut the dough into 2-inch squares with a knife or pizza cutter.

Bake the crackers for 10 to 14 minutes, until golden brown. Let the crackers cool on the baking sheets for 30 minutes, then serve.

Vegetables

Avocado Kale Salad ◉ 46

Primal Coleslaw ◉ 46

Bitter Dandelion Greens ◉ 47

Colorful Winter Salad ◉ 48

Cauliflower Rice ◉ 50

Rice Pilaf ◉ 51

Balsamic Rosemary Beets ◉ 53

Paleo "Potato" Leek Soup ◉ 54

Healing Vegetable Bisque ◉ 55

Roasted Broccoli ◉ 56

Sautéed Turnips ◉ 56

Stuffed Mushrooms ◉ 57

Sesame Noodles ◉ 58

Mushroom Lo Mein ◉ 60

Pad Thai ◉ 61

Twice-Baked Squash ◉ 62

Avocado Kale Salad

SERVES 4 ◉ Ⓜ Ⓥ

My younger son loves to whip up this family favorite for dinner—a good thing since kale is a super-food, full of nutrients and healthy phytochemicals. Massaging the kale makes it tender.

1 bunch kale, sliced crosswise into ¼-inch strips (about 4 cups)

2 tablespoons olive oil

1 tablespoon freshly squeezed lemon juice

1 very ripe avocado, diced into 1-inch cubes

½ teaspoon freshly ground black pepper

¼ teaspoon sea salt

In a large bowl, combine the kale, olive oil, and lemon juice and use your hands to massage the ingredients together until the kale is tender. Massage the avocado into the salad with your hands until it is completely mashed and mixed into the salad. Sprinkle with the pepper and salt, toss to combine, and serve.

Primal Coleslaw

SERVES 4 ◉ Ⓜ

Serve this coleslaw with Classic Salmon Burgers (page 76) and Dill Tartar Sauce (page 88) for a summertime barbecue. The result? A refreshing and satisfying meal.

1 small head green cabbage, grated (about 3 cups)

6 medium carrots, grated (about 3 cups)

½ cup Paleo Mayonnaise (page 88)

3 tablespoons apple cider vinegar

1 tablespoon honey

¼ teaspoon sea salt

In a large bowl, combine the cabbage and carrots. Add the mayonnaise, vinegar, honey, and salt, toss to combine, and serve.

Bitter Dandelion Greens

SERVES 4 ◌ Ⓜ Ⓥ

Bitter is one of the most underrated flavors in a modern society
fixated on sweet and salty; as a result, many people find them-
selves addicted to coffee, one of the few sources of bitterness
that's readily available. Dandelion greens are not only the king
of bitter greens, they are also fabulous for detoxifying the liver.
Serve as a side with scrambled eggs for breakfast or alongside
any dinner. See photo on page 74.

2 tablespoons olive oil
1 medium onion, finely chopped
    (about 1 cup)
1 bunch dandelion greens, stems
    discarded and sliced crosswise
    into 1-inch strips (about 4 cups)
$1/_8$ teaspoon sea salt

Heat the olive oil in a large skillet over
medium heat. Sauté the onion for 8 to
10 minutes, until soft and translucent.
Add the dandelion greens and sauté for
2 to 3 minutes, until wilted and tender.
Stir in the salt and serve.

Colorful Winter Salad

SERVES 4 ◉ Ⓜ Ⓥ

Made with purple cabbage, romaine lettuce, and carrots (all high in fiber, vitamin C, and vitamin A), this colorful salad will give you a rainbow full of nutrients in the dark of winter. To julienne your carrots quickly, use a julienne slicer—you can find this useful gadget online or at cookware stores. Or, you can simply slice the carrots into matchstick-size pieces.

1 small head purple cabbage, grated (about 3 cups)
1 small head romaine lettuce, grated (about 1 cup)
2 medium carrots, julienned (about 1 cup)
¼ cup Tahini Dressing (page 91)

In a large bowl, combine the cabbage, lettuce, and carrots. Toss with the Tahini Dressing and serve.

Colorful Winter Salad with > Tahini Dressing (page 91)

Cauliflower Rice

SERVES 4 ⊙ Ⓜ Ⓥ

When I gave up starchy rice, I didn't think I'd ever get to mop up
sauces in a plate of yumminess again. Then along came cauliflower
rice. Low in carbohydrates and high in nutrients, it's a wonderful
accompaniment to dishes such as Asian Stir-Fry (page 82) or Beef
with Broccoli (page 84). See photo on page 83.

3 tablespoons olive oil

1 medium onion, finely chopped
(about 1 cup)

4 stalks celery, finely chopped
(about 1 cup)

1 large head cauliflower, trimmed
and coarsely chopped

¼ teaspoon sea salt

Heat the olive oil in a large skillet over
medium heat. Sauté the onion for 8 to
10 minutes, until soft and translucent.
Add the celery and sauté for 5 minutes.

In a food processor, pulse the cauliflower until it is the texture of rice. Add
the cauliflower to the skillet, cover,
and cook for 15 to 20 minutes, stirring
occasionally, until soft. Stir in the salt
and serve.

Rice Pilaf

SERVES 4 ⊙ Ⓥ

This Paleo staple and über-healthy alternative to traditional rice is low in calories and, more importantly, rich in antioxidants. I've now made cauli-rice (as we call it in my house) in just about every way possible—this version is one of our favorites.

2 tablespoons coconut oil

1 medium onion, finely chopped (about 1 cup)

1 large head cauliflower, trimmed and coarsely chopped

1/4 cup currants

1/4 cup sliced almonds

1/2 teaspoon sea salt

Heat the coconut oil in a large skillet over medium heat. Sauté the onion for 8 to 10 minutes, until soft and translucent.

In a food processor, pulse the cauliflower until it is the texture of rice. Add the cauliflower to the skillet, cover, and cook for 15 to 20 minutes, stirring occasionally, until soft. Add the currants, almonds, and salt and cook for 1 to 2 minutes, stirring constantly, then serve.

Balsamic Rosemary Beets

SERVES 4 ⊙ (M) (V)

Beets are fabulous and far more nutritious than starchy white potatoes. After eating my balsamic-enhanced version, several friends have jumped onto the beet bandwagon.

4 medium beets, peeled and cut into
   1-inch cubes (about 4 cups)
1 tablespoon olive oil
1 tablespoon balsamic vinegar
1 tablespoon minced fresh rosemary
$1/2$ teaspoon freshly ground black pepper
$1/4$ teaspoon sea salt

Preheat the oven to 400°F.

In a medium bowl, combine the beets, olive oil, vinegar, rosemary, pepper, and salt. Transfer the beets to a 9 by 13-inch baking dish and cover with aluminum foil.

Bake for 45 minutes. Remove the foil and bake, uncovered, for 10 to 20 more minutes, until the beets are tender when pierced with a fork, then serve.

Paleo "Potato" Leek Soup

SERVES 4 ⊙ Ⓜ

Potato leek soup? Not so much. White potatoes don't agree with me. Leeks with creamy, ultrahealthy cauliflower? Absolutely. This vegetable has allowed me to reinvent many of my old favorite recipes.

2 tablespoons coconut oil

1 medium leek, white and green parts, thinly sliced (about 3 cups)

1 large head cauliflower, trimmed and coarsely chopped

6 cups chicken stock

$1/2$ teaspoon sea salt

$1/2$ teaspoon freshly ground black pepper

Heat the coconut oil in a large saucepan over medium heat. Sauté the leek for 10 to 15 minutes, until lightly browned. Add the cauliflower and sauté for about 15 minutes, until tender. Add the stock to the saucepan and bring to a boil. Lower the heat and simmer for 20 minutes. Remove from the heat and let cool for 15 minutes.

In a high-powered blender, carefully puree 2 cups of the soup at a time until very smooth, then transfer the soup to a clean saucepan.

Stir in the salt and pepper, reheat, and serve.

Healing Vegetable Bisque

SERVES 4 ⊙ Ⓜ

My friend Shila Wilson taught me how to make this amazingly healthy dish full of healing root vegetables. It's perfect on a winter night served with Rosemary Lemon Chicken (page 70) and a big helping of Avocado Kale Salad (page 46).

2 tablespoons olive oil

1 medium onion, chopped (about 1 cup)

4 medium carrots, chopped (about 2 cups)

1 medium daikon root, chopped (about 1 cup)

1 medium burdock root, chopped (about $1/2$ cup)

6 cups chicken stock

$3/4$ teaspoon sea salt

Heat the olive oil in a large saucepan over medium heat. Sauté the onion for 8 to 10 minutes, until soft and translucent. Add the carrots, daikon, and burdock and sauté for 15 to 20 minutes, until the vegetables start to brown. Add the stock to the saucepan and bring to a boil. Lower the heat and simmer for 30 minutes. Remove from the heat and let cool for 15 minutes.

In a high-powered blender, carefully puree 2 cups of the soup at a time until very smooth, then transfer the soup to a clean saucepan.

Stir in the salt, reheat, and serve.

Roasted Broccoli

SERVES 4 ◉ Ⓜ Ⓥ

This easy dish is both delicious and elegant. It's equally wonderful for an everyday meal or special occasion. Serve with Marinated Flank Steak (page 81) or Mustard Salmon Fillet (page 75).

3 heads broccoli, sliced into 3-inch
    spears (about 6 cups)
2 tablespoons olive oil
$1/2$ teaspoon sea salt

Preheat the oven to 400°F.

    In a large bowl, use your hands to toss together the broccoli, olive oil, and salt. Spread the broccoli in a single layer on 2 baking sheets.

    Bake for 15 to 20 minutes, until the broccoli is crisp-tender and beginning to brown. Let cool for 5 minutes, then serve.

Sautéed Turnips

SERVES 4 ◉ Ⓜ

Not your grandmother's turnips, this fresh take on a staid old vegetable will ignite your love of this healthy root and convert even the most hardened turnip haters. My friend Deb, of the website Revive Organizing, taught me how to make this dish, which is based on a recipe developed by Jane Brody years ago.

1 tablespoon coconut oil
1 tablespoon honey
4 medium turnips, chopped into
    $1/4$-inch cubes (about 4 cups)
$1/2$ teaspoon freshly ground black
    pepper
1 tablespoon minced fresh flat-leaf
    parsley

Heat the coconut oil and honey in a large skillet over medium heat. Add the turnips and pepper, cover, and cook for about 10 minutes, stirring frequently to prevent sticking, until the turnips are fork tender and golden brown. Sprinkle with parsley and then serve.

Stuffed Mushrooms

MAKES 24 MUSHROOMS   ◉ Ⓜ

I've enjoyed stuffed mushrooms since I was a teenager, though I used to make them with cheese. Now that I avoid dairy, this dish is the perfect high-protein replacement.

24 white mushrooms, each 2 inches across, stems removed and reserved

$1/2$ pound organic ground pork or beef

$1/2$ cup minced fresh flat-leaf parsley

4 shallots, finely chopped (about $1/4$ cup)

1 tablespoon minced fresh garlic

1 tablespoon minced fresh rosemary

1 large egg

$3/4$ teaspoon sea salt

$1/2$ teaspoon freshly ground black pepper

Preheat the oven to 400°F. Line a baking sheet with parchment paper.

In a food processor, pulse together the mushroom stems, ground pork, parsley, shallots, garlic, rosemary, egg, salt, and pepper until combined, being careful not to overprocess. Spoon 1 heaping tablespoon of the filling into each mushroom cap and place on the prepared baking sheet.

Bake for 30 to 40 minutes, until the mushrooms are tender and the filling is cooked through and browned, then serve.

Sesame Noodles

SERVES 4

My friend Kelly, who writes about gluten-free living on the Spunky Coconut website, loves sesame noodles, and so do I. We both like the slight crunch of this healthy, low-calorie dish made of sea vegetables. For a main dish, serve with Sesame Fish Sticks (page 72) or Honey Lemon Chicken (page 65).

1 (12-ounce) package kelp noodles

$\frac{1}{4}$ cup roasted almond butter, at room temperature

1 tablespoon toasted sesame oil

1 tablespoon ume plum vinegar

1 tablespoon honey

Sesame seeds, for garnish

Soak the kelp noodles in a bowl of hot water for 30 minutes. Drain the noodles and rinse thoroughly.

In a small bowl, whisk together the almond butter, sesame oil, vinegar, and honey. Add the noodles and toss to combine. Sprinkle with sesame seeds and serve.

Sesame Noodles with >
Honey Lemon Chicken (page 65)

Mushroom Lo Mein

SERVES 4 ⊙ Ⓝ Ⓥ

If you miss Chinese food, this dish—made with healthy kelp noodles—will hit the spot. Serve with Rosemary Lemon Chicken (page 70), Marinated Flank Steak (page 81), or Sesame Fish Sticks (page 72) for an Asian-themed dinner.

1 (12-ounce) package kelp noodles
2 tablespoons coconut oil
1 medium onion, thinly sliced (about 1 cup)
1 medium head savoy or napa cabbage, thinly sliced (about 4 cups)
1 cup water
8 ounces shiitake mushrooms, stemmed and thinly sliced (about 2 cups)
1 teaspoon toasted sesame oil
1 teaspoon minced fresh garlic
¼ teaspoon sea salt

Soak the kelp noodles in a bowl of hot water for 30 minutes. Drain the noodles and rinse thoroughly.

Heat the coconut oil in a large skillet over medium heat. Sauté the onion for 8 to 10 minutes, until soft and translucent. Add the cabbage and water and cook, covered, until the cabbage is soft, about 10 minutes. Add the mushrooms and sauté for about 5 minutes, until tender. Stir in the sesame oil, garlic, and salt.

Stir in the kelp noodles and cook for about 5 minutes, until heated through and the flavors are combined, then serve.

Pad Thai

SERVES 4 ◦ **Ⓥ**

I wouldn't have thought of making pad thai into a Paleo dish, but then I saw a post by Melissa Joulwan on the website the Clothes Make the Girl. That was all it took to change my mind. I serve my version of Paleo pad thai with leftover chicken, beef, or seafood or with freshly made Rosemary Lemon Chicken (page 70).

1 medium spaghetti squash, seeds removed and cut into quarters (about 4 cups)

3 tablespoons coconut oil

1 medium onion, finely chopped (about 1 cup)

1 head broccoli, chopped (about 2 cups)

2 heads baby bok choy, sliced crosswise into 1-inch strips (about 1$^1/_2$ cups)

6 scallions, white and green parts, thinly sliced (about $^3/_4$ cup)

$^1/_2$ cup minced fresh cilantro

1 cup cashews, toasted and chopped

Tangy "Peanut" Sauce (page 90)

Place a metal steamer basket in a large pot and add 3 inches of water. Steam the spaghetti squash in the basket for 20 minutes, or until tender when pierced with a fork. Remove the spaghetti squash from the basket; when cool enough to handle, scoop the spaghetti squash out of the skin.

Heat the coconut oil in a large skillet over medium heat. Sauté the onion for 8 to 10 minutes, until soft and translucent. Add the broccoli and sauté for about 10 minutes, until tender. Stir in the bok choy and sauté for 3 to 4 minutes, until wilted. Add the squash to the skillet, stir briefly to incorporate, then add the scallions and cilantro.

Top with the toasted cashews and Tangy "Peanut" Sauce and serve.

Twice-Baked Squash

SERVES 4 ◎ Ⓜ

Squash, carrots, and other orange vegetables are the perfect
source of beta-carotene, a form of vitamin A, which, if eaten in
large amounts, can give your skin a funny orange tinge. When my
younger son was a toddler, he turned orange from eating so much
squash—my fault, as I like it just as much as he does. Now that
you've been warned, try not to eat this velvety smooth casserole
all by yourself.

1 medium butternut squash, halved
    and seeded

1/2 cup water

2 large eggs

1/2 cup freshly squeezed orange juice

2 tablespoons coconut oil, melted
    over very low heat

10 drops vanilla crème stevia

1 teaspoon ground cinnamon

1/4 teaspoon ground nutmeg

1/4 teaspoon sea salt

Preheat the oven to 350°F.

Place the squash cut side down in
a 13 by 9-inch baking dish and add the
water. Bake for 50 to 60 minutes, until
the squash is very tender and falling
apart.

Remove the skin from the squash
and discard. In a high-powered blender,
puree the squash, eggs, orange juice,
coconut oil, stevia, cinnamon, nutmeg,
and salt until very smooth.

Transfer the mixture to an 8-inch
square baking dish and bake for
50 to 60 minutes, until lightly browned,
then serve.

Entrées

Honey Lemon Chicken ⊚ 65

Chicken Gumbo ⊚ 66

Chicken Salad ⊚ 67

Chicken Marbella ⊚ 68

Rosemary Lemon Chicken ⊚ 70

Paleo Shepherd's Pie ⊚ 71

Sesame Fish Sticks ⊚ 72

Salmon Salad ⊚ 73

Mustard Salmon Fillet ⊚ 75

Classic Salmon Burgers ⊚ 76

Greek Turkey Burgers ⊚ 77

Bacon Tart ⊚ 79

Green Frittata ⊚ 80

Marinated Flank Steak ⊚ 81

Asian Stir-Fry ⊚ 82

Beef with Broccoli ⊚ 84

Honey Lemon Chicken

SERVES 4 ◉ Ⓜ

Serve this chicken at the table in the baking dish so your family can enjoy the drippings. My younger son likes to smother his steamed broccoli in them, while I eat the cooked garlic on Paleo Bread (page 34).

1 whole chicken, 2 to 3 pounds
2 tablespoons olive oil
2 tablespoons honey
1 tablespoon sea salt
3 lemons
2 medium onions
1 head garlic

Preheat the oven to 350°F.

Rinse the chicken and pat dry. Place the chicken, breast side down, in a 13 by 9-inch baking dish.

Drizzle the chicken with the olive oil and honey, sprinkle with the salt, and stuff with 1 of the whole lemons. Cut the remaining 2 lemons in half and place in the corners of the baking dish. Cut the onions in half (leaving the skin on) and place alongside the lemon halves. Break the head of garlic apart (leaving the skin on) and scatter the cloves around the baking dish.

Bake the chicken for 50 to 60 minutes, until the skin is well browned. Increase the heat to 450°F, turn the chicken breast side up, and bake for about 15 more minutes, until an instant-read thermometer inserted into the thigh reads 170°F to 180°F.

Remove the chicken from the oven. Carve the chicken, drizzle with the pan juices, and serve.

Chicken Gumbo

SERVES 4 ⊙ Ⓧ

Although gumbo, a thick stew filled with meat and vegetables, is traditionally spicy, I avoid spicy foods, so I use vegetables and herbs to get this dish to pop. If you want some heat, add cayenne and chili powder to take it to the next level.

1 pound boneless, skinless chicken breasts

2 tablespoons coconut oil

1 medium onion, finely chopped (about 1 cup)

2 stalks celery, finely chopped (about 1/2 cup)

2 medium carrots, thinly sliced (about 1 cup)

1 medium turnip, chopped into 1/4-inch cubes (about 1 cup)

4 ounces cremini or white mushrooms, stemmed and thinly sliced (about 1 cup)

1/2 teaspoon sea salt

1/2 cup minced fresh flat-leaf parsley

2 tablespoons arrowroot powder

1 cup chicken stock

Cauliflower Rice (page 50), for serving

Rinse the chicken and pat dry. Cut into 1/2-inch cubes and transfer to a plate.

Heat the coconut oil in a large skillet over medium heat. Sauté the onion for 8 to 10 minutes, until soft and translucent. Add the celery, carrots, turnips, mushrooms, and salt. Cover and cook for 10 to 15 minutes, stirring occasionally, until the vegetables are tender. Add the chicken, cover, and cook, stirring occasionally, for about 5 minutes, until the chicken is cooked through. Stir in the parsley.

In a small bowl, dissolve the arrowroot powder in the stock, stirring until thoroughly combined. Raise the heat under the chicken-vegetable mixture to high, then add the arrowroot mixture. Cook, stirring constantly, for 2 to 3 minutes, until the sauce thickens and becomes glossy. Serve over the Cauliflower Rice.

Chicken Salad

SERVES 4 ⊙ Ⓜ

Because this recipe uses leftover chicken, it's a great dish to make when you are short on time and craving a superhealthy high-protein meal. My boys devour this chicken salad for dinner on hot summer nights. I like it as much as they do.

2 cups cooked shredded chicken
8 stalks celery, finely chopped (about 2 cups)
2 Granny Smith apples, cored and diced into 1-inch cubes
1 cup minced fresh flat-leaf parsley
1/4 cup Paleo Mayonnaise (page 88)
1/4 cup Dijon mustard
1/4 teaspoon sea salt
1/4 teaspoon freshly ground black pepper
1 head romaine lettuce, sliced crosswise into 1-inch strips (about 4 cups)

In a large bowl, combine the chicken, celery, apples, parsley, and mayonnaise. Stir in the mustard, salt, and pepper, tossing to combine.

Serve over the romaine lettuce.

Chicken Marbella

SERVES 6 ◉ Ⓜ

This classic recipe hails from the *Silver Palate Cookbook*. I've altered it by using boneless chicken breasts rather than thighs and removing the sugar. Back when I was attending college in New York City, I used to walk by the Silver Palate shop on my long strolls through the Upper West Side. Not much into cooking back then, I don't think I ever went in.

2 pounds boneless, skinless chicken breasts
1 cup prunes, pitted and halved
2 cups green olives, pitted
1/2 cup honey
1/4 cup olive oil
1/4 cup capers
2 tablespoons apple cider vinegar
2 tablespoons minced fresh garlic
2 tablespoons dried oregano
3 bay leaves
1 teaspoon sea salt
1/2 teaspoon freshly ground black pepper
1/4 cup minced fresh flat-leaf parsley

Rinse the chicken and pat dry. Cut into 2-inch cubes.

In a large bowl, combine the prunes, olives, honey, olive oil, capers, vinegar, garlic, oregano, bay leaves, salt, and pepper. Add the chicken cubes to the bowl and toss to coat completely. Cover and refrigerate for 2 hours up to overnight.

Preheat the oven to 350°F.

Transfer the chicken and marinade to a 13 by 9-inch baking dish, arranging the chicken in a single layer. Bake for 40 to 50 minutes, until the edges of the chicken pieces are golden brown. Sprinkle the chicken with the parsley and serve.

Rosemary Lemon Chicken

SERVES 4 ⊙ Ⓜ

We make this chicken at least once a week—it goes with every-thing. This recipe is adapted from one by the incredible Ina Garten.

1 pound boneless, skinless chicken
   breasts
$1/3$ cup olive oil
$1/3$ cup freshly squeezed lemon juice
$1^1/2$ teaspoons minced fresh rosemary
1 teaspoon sea salt
$1/2$ teaspoon freshly ground black pepper

Rinse the chicken and pat dry. Cut the chicken breasts in half lengthwise.

In a medium bowl, combine the olive oil, lemon juice, rosemary, salt, and pepper to make the marinade. Pour the marinade into an 8-inch square baking dish, then add the chicken to the dish. Cover and refrigerate for 3 to 6 hours.

Heat the grill and cook the chicken breasts for 3 to 5 minutes on each side, until cooked through. Let the chicken cool for 5 minutes, then serve.

Paleo Shepherd's Pie

SERVES 6 ⊙ Ⓜ

Shepherd's pie (also known as cottage pie), a savory dish popular in England, dates back to the 1870s. It's traditionally made of minced meat (often lamb, hence the name) and topped with mashed potatoes; in the United States it is more often made with ground beef. If you want the topping to get browned, go with the longer cooking time. I like the edges of my shepherd's pie slightly burned.

3 large heads cauliflower, trimmed and coarsely chopped

4 tablespoons olive oil

2 medium onions, finely chopped (about 2 cups)

4 medium carrots, diced (about 2 cups)

4 stalks celery, diced (about 1 cup)

1 pound organic ground beef

1 cup chicken stock

1 teaspoon freshly ground black pepper

$\frac{1}{2}$ teaspoon sea salt

Preheat the oven to 350°F.

Steam the cauliflower until it is very tender, then set aside.

Heat 2 tablespoons of the olive oil in a large skillet over medium heat. Sauté the onions for 8 to 10 minutes, until soft and translucent. Add the carrots and celery and sauté for about 10 minutes, until soft. Add the beef to the skillet, breaking it up with a wooden spoon, and sauté for 5 to 7 minutes, until brown. Add the stock and cook down until half of the liquid has evaporated, 7 to 8 minutes. Stir in the pepper and salt, then transfer the mixture to a 13 by 9-inch baking dish.

In a food processor, pulse together the cauliflower and the remaining 2 tablespoons of olive oil until smooth. Spread the mashed cauliflower on top of the beef mixture.

Bake for 70 to 90 minutes, until browned around the edges. Let cool for 10 minutes, then serve.

Sesame Fish Sticks

SERVES 4

Healthy fish sticks coated with crunchy sesame seeds make fun finger food for children—and provide sophisticated flavor for adults. Serve leftover fish sticks the next day on Sesame Noodles (page 58) for a quick yet satisfyingly tasty meal.

1 pound wild cod fillet
2 large eggs
1 cup sesame seeds
$^1\!/_2$ cup blanched almond flour
1 tablespoon coconut flour
$^1\!/_2$ teaspoon sea salt
$^1\!/_4$ cup olive oil

Rinse the cod and pat dry. Cut into $1^1\!/_2$-inch-wide strips.

In a medium bowl, whisk the eggs. In a separate bowl, stir together the sesame seeds, almond flour, coconut flour, and salt. Dip each cod strip into the eggs, then coat with the sesame mixture.

Heat 2 tablespoons of the olive oil in a large skillet over medium-high heat. Cook half of the fish sticks for 3 to 5 minutes per side, until well browned. Transfer to a paper towel–lined plate.

Repeat the process with the remaining oil and fish, then serve.

Salmon Salad

SERVES 4 ⊙ Ⓜ

I stopped eating tuna years ago when I discovered that I had mercury toxicity, since tuna can be high in this toxin. A wonderful replacement for tuna salad, this dish is delicious served on toasted grain-free Bagels (page 19). Leftover cooked salmon also works very well in this recipe.

1 pound skinless wild salmon fillet

$1/4$ cup Paleo Mayonnaise (page 88)

$1/4$ cup Dijon mustard

2 stalks celery, finely chopped (about $1/2$ cup)

$1/4$ cup minced fresh dill

1 shallot, minced (about 1 tablespoon)

$1/2$ teaspoon freshly ground black pepper

$1/4$ teaspoon sea salt

1 head romaine lettuce, sliced crosswise into 1-inch strips (about 4 cups)

Preheat the oven to 400°F.

Rinse the salmon and pat dry. Place the salmon in a 13 by 9-inch baking dish. Bake for 15 to 20 minutes, until the salmon is cooked through. Let cool for 10 minutes, then flake with a fork.

In a large bowl, stir together the salmon, mayonnaise, and mustard. Add the celery, dill, shallot, pepper, and salt and mix thoroughly.

Serve over the romaine lettuce.

Mustard Salmon Fillet

SERVES 4 ⊙ Ⓜ

My friend Deb, from the website Revive Organizing, taught me to make this simple yet elegant baked salmon. Because it takes very little time to prepare and always impresses, it's her go-to dish for guests.

1½ pounds wild salmon fillet
1 cup Dijon mustard

Preheat the oven to 400°F. Rinse the salmon and pat dry. Place the salmon skin side down in a 13 by 9-inch baking dish. Spread the mustard over the salmon.

Bake for 15 to 20 minutes, until cooked through, then serve.

< Mustard Salmon Fillet with Bitter Dandelion Greens (page 47)

Classic Salmon Burgers

MAKES 6 BURGERS ⊙ Ⓜ

Because it is high in heart-healthy omega-3 fatty acids, we eat salmon for dinner at least once a week. I purchase wild salmon; farmed salmon is often treated with antibiotics to promote growth, and with artificial color to enhance its appearance. Like livestock, farmed salmon is also often fed a diet of cornmeal, soy, and genetically modified oils. This recipe is based on one of my favorites from the magazine *Fine Cooking*. The difference? I've increased the amount of capers, mustard, and other accents in this dish to mask the flavor of fish that my boys tend to eschew.

1½ pounds skinless wild salmon fillet
4 shallots, finely chopped (about ¼ cup)
¼ cup chopped capers
2 tablespoons Dijon mustard
1 teaspoon sea salt
1 teaspoon freshly ground black pepper
2 tablespoons olive oil
Dill Tartar Sauce (page 88)

Rinse the salmon and pat dry. Cut into ¼-inch cubes.

In a food processor, pulse the salmon cubes until coarsely chopped. Transfer the salmon to a bowl, then stir in the shallots, capers, mustard, salt, and pepper. Using your hands, form the mixture into 6 patties, each about 3½ inches in diameter.

Heat the olive oil in a large skillet over medium heat. Cook the patties for 3 to 5 minutes per side, until golden brown around the edges. Transfer the patties to a paper towel–lined plate, then serve with Dill Tartar Sauce.

Greek Turkey Burgers

MAKES 6 BURGERS ⊙ Ⓜ

I've been to Greece twice, once with my parents when I was a teenager and again with my friend Mary in my twenties. Both times I enjoyed the amazingly fresh flavors of Greek food, which these burgers evoke.

1 pound organic ground turkey

1 medium zucchini, shredded (about 1 cup)

1 small onion, minced (about ½ cup)

½ cup minced fresh flat-leaf parsley

2 large eggs

3 tablespoons olive oil

1 tablespoon dried oregano

1 tablespoon Spice Hunter Greek Seasoning

1 teaspoon freshly ground black pepper

½ teaspoon sea salt

In a large bowl, combine the ground turkey, zucchini, onion, parsley, eggs, and 1 tablespoon of the olive oil. Add the oregano, Greek seasoning, pepper, and salt, using your hands to thoroughly mix the ingredients. Form the mixture into 6 patties, each about 3 inches in diameter.

Heat the remaining 2 tablespoons of olive oil in a large skillet over medium heat. Cook the patties for 4 to 6 minutes per side, until golden brown around the edges. Transfer the patties to a paper towel–lined plate, then serve.

Bacon Tart

SERVES 6

This versatile high-protein tart can be made with regular bacon or turkey bacon. Serve it for dinner with a salad dressed with my eggless Caesar Dressing (page 87), or wow your guests with this elegantly simple dish at a festive brunch.

1 pound organic bacon

8 scallions, white and green parts, thinly sliced (about 1 cup)

8 large eggs

$1/2$ teaspoon freshly ground black pepper

$1/4$ teaspoon sea salt

1 prebaked Shallot Tart Crust (page 102)

Preheat the oven to 350°F.

In a large skillet, cook the bacon over medium-high heat until lightly browned, 4 to 6 minutes. Remove the bacon from the skillet and, when cool enough to handle, mince. Pour off and discard the fat from the skillet. Return the minced bacon to the skillet, add the scallions, and sauté for 3 minutes.

In a large bowl, whisk together the eggs, pepper, and salt. Stir in the bacon and scallions, then pour the mixture into the prepared crust.

Bake the tart for 25 to 30 minutes, until browned around the edges and cooked through. Let cool for 20 minutes, then serve.

< Bacon Tart with Shallot Tart Crust (page 102)

Green Frittata

SERVES 8 ⊙ Ⓜ

Cooking the eggs in this frittata slowly gives them a delicate texture and wonderful flavor. We often have this dish for a quick dinner with Salsa Verde (page 89). It's also perfect to pack for a picnic. See photo on page 30.

1 tablespoon olive oil
1 medium onion, chopped (about 1 cup)
1 head broccoli, sliced into 3-inch spears (about 2 cups)
½ bunch kale, sliced crosswise into ¼-inch strips (about 2 cups)
10 large eggs, whisked
½ teaspoon sea salt
½ teaspoon freshly ground black pepper

Heat the olive oil in a 9-inch skillet over medium heat. Sauté the onion for 8 to 10 minutes, until soft and translucent. Add the broccoli and sauté for about 10 minutes, until crisp-tender. Add the kale and sauté for about 3 minutes, until wilted.

Pour the eggs over the vegetables, tilting the skillet to distribute them evenly, then sprinkle with the salt and pepper. Decrease the heat to low, cover, and cook for 20 to 30 minutes, or until the eggs are set.

Cut the frittata into 8 wedges and serve.

Marinated Flank Steak

SERVES 4 ⊙ Ⓜ

Less expensive than cuts such as rib eye or sirloin, flank steak is lean and somewhat tough, so it lends itself quite well to marinating, which tenderizes it. Make sure not to overcook it, as these thin steaks can dry out very easily.

1½ cups freshly squeezed orange juice
¼ cup ume plum vinegar
1 tablespoon toasted sesame oil
1 tablespoon peeled and minced fresh ginger
1 teaspoon minced fresh garlic
1 pound organic flank steak

In a small bowl, combine the orange juice, vinegar, sesame oil, ginger, and garlic to make the marinade. Pour the marinade into an 11 by 7-inch baking dish, then place the flank steak in the dish. Marinate for 4 to 8 hours in the refrigerator, turning it halfway through the marinating time if desired.

Remove the steak from the refrigerator and let rest for 15 minutes. Heat a large skillet over high heat. Cook the steak for 2 to 4 minutes on each side until an instant-read thermometer inserted into the thickest part of the steak registers 130°F for medium-rare, or until cooked to your desired doneness.

Let the steak rest for 5 to 10 minutes. Cut against the grain into ½-inch-thick slices and serve.

Asian Stir-Fry

SERVES 4 ⊚ Ⓜ

Although stir-fries are traditionally made in a wok, I use a 12-inch skillet, which works just as well. The key is having a large surface area for cooking the bounty of vegetables in this Asian-inspired medley of sesame-spiced ingredients. Serve over Cauliflower Rice (page 50).

1 pound boneless, skinless chicken breasts

2 tablespoons coconut oil

1 medium onion, finely chopped (about 1 cup)

2 heads broccoli, sliced into 3-inch spears (about 4 cups)

2 medium carrots, sliced (about 1 cup)

2 heads baby bok choy, sliced crosswise into 1-inch strips (about 1¹/₂ cups)

4 ounces shiitake mushrooms, stemmed and thinly sliced (about 1 cup)

1 small zucchini, sliced (about 1 cup)

¹/₂ teaspoon sea salt

1¹/₂ cups water

2 tablespoons arrowroot powder

2 tablespoons toasted sesame oil

2 tablespoons ume plum vinegar

1 tablespoon honey

Rinse the chicken and pat dry. Cut into 1-inch cubes and transfer to a plate.

Heat the coconut oil in a large skillet over medium heat. Sauté the onion for 8 to 10 minutes, until soft and translucent. Add the broccoli, carrots, and chicken and sauté for 10 minutes until almost tender. Add the bok choy, mushrooms, zucchini, and salt and sauté for 5 minutes. Add 1 cup of the water, cover the skillet, and cook for about 10 minutes, until the vegetables are wilted.

In a small bowl, dissolve the arrowroot powder in the remaining ¹/₂ cup of water, stirring until thoroughly combined. Add the arrowroot mixture to the vegetables and cook for 2 to 3 minutes, stirring constantly, until the sauce thickens and becomes glossy. Stir in the sesame oil, vinegar, and honey, then serve.

Asian Stir-Fry with Cauliflower Rice (page 50) >

Beef with Broccoli

SERVES 4 ⊙ Ⓜ

I turned to one of my favorite websites, Simply Recipes, for inspiration when creating this dish. I've incorporated parts of the method featured on that site, but I've changed the ingredients to make the dish Paleo. Serve as a one-pot meal, or make Cauliflower Rice (page 50) to go with it.

1 pound organic sirloin steak

¼ cup freshly squeezed orange juice

2 tablespoons ume plum vinegar

1 tablespoon minced fresh garlic

1 tablespoon arrowroot powder

2 tablespoons coconut oil

1 medium onion, finely chopped (about 1 cup)

3 heads broccoli, sliced into 3-inch spears (about 6 cups)

Slice the steak thinly across the grain and place the slices in an 8-inch square baking dish. In a small bowl, combine the orange juice, vinegar, garlic, and arrowroot powder to make the marinade. Drizzle the marinade over the steak and refrigerate for 15 minutes.

Heat the coconut oil in a large skillet over medium heat. Sauté the onion for 8 to 10 minutes, until soft and translucent. While the onion is sautéing, steam the broccoli for 8 to 10 minutes, or until crisp-tender, then remove from the steamer and set aside.

Add the beef to the skillet, spreading it out in a single layer. Sauté for about 1 minute on each side, until cooked through.

Add the steamed broccoli and marinade to the skillet. Cook, stirring constantly, for about 3 minutes, until the sauce thickens and becomes glossy, then serve.

Condiments, Spreads, and Toppings

Basil Cream Sauce ◎ 86

Caesar Dressing ◎ 87

Dill Tartar Sauce ◎ 88

Paleo Mayonnaise ◎ 88

Roasted Garlic ◎ 89

Salsa Verde ◎ 89

Tangy "Peanut" Sauce ◎ 90

Vegan Pesto Rustico ◎ 90

Very Dijon Salad Dressing ◎ 91

Tahini Dressing ◎ 91

Cherry Berry Syrup ◎ 92

Coconut Whipped Cream ◎ 93

Strawberry Applesauce ◎ 94

Basil Cream Sauce

MAKES 1½ CUPS ⊙ Ⓜ Ⓥ

I like to toss this creamy sauce with a package of raw kelp noodles, ¼ cup minced fresh basil, and ¼ cup chopped toasted cashews. You can also use it as a dipping sauce for vegetables and meats. Serve with Rosemary Lemon Chicken (page 70) for the perfect lunch or dinner. Be sure to refrigerate the coconut milk (see page 11) in advance of making the sauce.

1 cup coconut milk fat (scooped off the top of 2 cans of coconut milk)
1 tablespoon coconut cream concentrate or coconut butter
1 tablespoon ume plum vinegar
1 tablespoon freshly squeezed lime juice
½ cup coarsely chopped basil
1 teaspoon peeled and minced fresh ginger

In a high-powered blender, puree the coconut milk fat, coconut cream concentrate, vinegar, and lime juice until smooth. Add the basil and ginger and blend until thoroughly combined.

Use right away or store in a glass jar in the refrigerator for up to 2 days.

Caesar Dressing

MAKES 1½ CUPS ⊙ Ⓜ

This recipe for eggless Caesar salad dressing is based on one from *Bon Appétit*, where I also found the unique idea to serve it over kale. Kale Caesar is now my family's favorite salad, which comes in handy each summer when my garden is in full swing and we eat kale with dinner on a nightly basis. Of course, this dressing is delightful over romaine lettuce or in a chicken Caesar salad as well.

1 cup olive oil
2 tablespoons freshly squeezed
   lemon juice
2 tablespoons anchovies
2 tablespoons Dijon mustard
1 teaspoon minced fresh garlic
½ teaspoon sea salt
½ teaspoon freshly ground black
   pepper

In a high-powered blender, puree the olive oil, lemon juice, anchovies, mustard, garlic, salt, and pepper until smooth.

Use right away or store in a glass jar in the refrigerator for up to 3 days.

Dill Tartar Sauce

MAKES 1 CUP ⦿ Ⓜ

Full of summery dill flavor, this sauce is delectable on Classic Salmon Burgers (page 76).

1/2 cup Paleo Mayonnaise (opposite)
2 dill pickles, finely chopped (about 1/2 cup)
2 tablespoons minced fresh dill
1/2 teaspoon firmly packed lemon zest
1/4 teaspoon sea salt
1/4 teaspoon freshly ground black pepper

In a small bowl, stir together the mayonnaise, pickles, dill, lemon zest, salt, and pepper.

Use right away or store in a glass jar in the refrigerator for up to 2 days.

Paleo Mayonnaise

MAKES 1 CUP ⦿ Ⓜ

Be sure to use a very mild extra-virgin olive oil when making this mayonnaise. If you use something with a stronger flavor, the mayo will become bitter. After testing several brands, I recommend Lapas Organic Extra Virgin Olive Oil for the best results.

1 large egg
1 tablespoon apple cider vinegar
1/4 teaspoon sea salt
1 cup olive oil

In a high-powered blender, blend the egg, vinegar, and salt until smooth, about 10 seconds.

Place the olive oil in a liquid measuring cup with a spout. With the blender running, slowly pour in the olive oil in a fine stream. Continue blending until mixture thickens to the consistency of mayonnaise.

Use right away or store in a glass jar in the refrigerator for up to 3 days.

Roasted Garlic

SERVES 4 ⊙ Ⓜ Ⓥ

As it's roasted, garlic takes on a sweet flavor. Serve over toasted Paleo Bread (page 34), or Garlic Crackers (page 43) to ward off vampires.

2 heads garlic
1/4 cup olive oil
1/8 teaspoon sea salt

Preheat the oven to 400°F.

Using a sharp knife, chop off the top 1/2 inch from each head of garlic (leaving the skin on), then place the heads in a 1-pint baking dish. Drizzle with olive oil, then sprinkle with the salt.

Bake, covered, for 30 to 40 minutes, until the garlic is fork tender. Let the garlic cool for 10 minutes, scoop the cloves from the skin, then spread on bread or crackers.

Salsa Verde

MAKES 1 1/2 CUPS ⊙ Ⓜ Ⓥ

I first ate salsa verde at one of my favorite restaurants, Oak, in Boulder. This is my version of their amazingly fresh and healthy recipe. Serve over Marinated Flank Steak (page 81). See photo on page 30.

1 cup olive oil
1 bunch flat-leaf parsley, coarsely chopped (about 1 1/2 cups)
1/2 bunch cilantro, coarsely chopped (about 3/4 cup)
2 sprigs tarragon
1 tablespoon firmly packed lemon zest
1 teaspoon sea salt
1 teaspoon freshly ground black pepper

In a high-powered blender, puree the olive oil, parsley, cilantro, and tarragon until very smooth. Blend in the lemon zest, salt, and pepper until thoroughly combined.

Use right away or store in a glass jar in the refrigerator for up to 24 hours.

Tangy "Peanut" Sauce

MAKES 1 CUP ◉ Ⓥ

This rich, tangy sauce can top off Pad Thai (page 61), kelp noodles, or steamed vegetables. My version, which uses almond butter instead of peanuts, is based on Melissa Joulwan's Sunshine Sauce, which can be found on her website the Clothes Make the Girl.

2 tablespoons freshly squeezed lime juice
1 tablespoon peeled and minced fresh ginger
1 teaspoon minced fresh garlic
1 teaspoon ume plum vinegar
$1/4$ cup roasted almond butter
$1/2$ cup coconut milk

In a high-powered blender, puree the lime juice, ginger, garlic, and vinegar until very smooth. Blend in the almond butter and coconut milk until thoroughly combined.

Use right away or store in a glass jar in the refrigerator for up to 3 days.

Vegan Pesto Rustico

MAKES 2 CUPS ◉ Ⓥ

I serve this pesto on Garlic Crackers (page 43); my younger son likes to eat it straight out of the bowl.

1 cup minced fresh basil
$1/2$ cup pine nuts
$1/2$ cup walnuts
$1/4$ cup olive oil
1 teaspoon minced fresh garlic
$1/2$ teaspoon freshly ground black pepper
$1/4$ teaspoon sea salt

Place the basil in a bowl and set aside.

In a skillet over medium heat, toast the pine nuts and walnuts for 10 minutes, until golden brown. Place the nuts on a cutting board and gently use the bottom of a glass jar to crush them until they are the texture of coarse gravel.

Add the nuts to the bowl with the basil and stir in the olive oil, garlic, pepper, and salt until thoroughly combined, then serve.

Very Dijon Salad Dressing

MAKES ³/₄ CUP ◌ Ⓜ Ⓥ

My boys are great about eating their greens. One trick I have up my sleeve is to rotate homemade salad dressings often so they don't get bored. Serve over raw kale, romaine lettuce, or mixed salad greens. You can also use this dressing as a marinade for fish or chicken.

½ cup olive oil
2 tablespoons apple cider vinegar
2 tablespoons Dijon mustard
6 drops stevia

In a high-powered blender, process the olive oil, vinegar, mustard, and stevia until smooth.

Use right away or store in a glass jar in the refrigerator for up to 3 days.

Tahini Dressing

MAKES 2 CUPS ◌ Ⓜ Ⓥ

Tahini is made from calcium-rich sesame seeds, so I try to serve this superfood to my children as often as possible. Use this dressing on the Colorful Winter Salad (page 48), or serve it as a dip with veggie sticks for a healthy afternoon snack. You can also serve it over kale, romaine lettuce, or mixed salad greens. See photo on page 49.

½ cup roasted tahini
½ cup water
¼ cup freshly squeezed lemon juice
2 tablespoons olive oil
1 teaspoon sea salt

In a high-powered blender, puree the tahini, water, lemon juice, olive oil, and salt until very smooth.

Use right away or store in a glass jar in the refrigerator for up to 3 days.

Cherry Berry Syrup

MAKES 4 CUPS ● SWEETNESS: MEDIUM ● Ⓜ Ⓥ

Prepare this syrup in advance, so that it has time to thicken, and then serve with Paleo Pancakes (page 22) or Crepes (page 23). With no added sugar, this recipe is a healthy version of the super-sweet Smucker's syrup I indulged in growing up.

1 (10-ounce) bag frozen cherries
1 (8-ounce) bag frozen blueberries
1 cup apple juice
$\frac{1}{8}$ teaspoon stevia
1 tablespoon arrowroot powder
$\frac{1}{4}$ cup water

In a saucepan over medium heat, bring the cherries, blueberries, apple juice, and stevia to a boil. Lower the heat and simmer for about 10 minutes, until the fruit is soft.

In a small bowl, dissolve the arrowroot powder in the water, stirring until thoroughly combined. Raise the heat to high, add the arrowroot mixture to the fruit, and cook, whisking constantly, until the mixture thickens and becomes glossy, about 1 minute. Let the sauce cool and thicken for 10 minutes before serving.

Use right away or store in a glass jar in the refrigerator for up to 3 days.

Coconut Whipped Cream

MAKES 1 CUP ● SWEETNESS: LOW ● Ⓜ

This dairy-free whipped cream recipe calls for full-fat canned coconut milk. The fat is what makes the recipe creamy and luscious; light coconut milk won't work and results in a watery mess. Serve over Upside-Down Apple Tartlets (page 101) or Peach Cherry Crisp (page 98). See photo on page 100.

1 (13-ounce) can Thai Kitchen
    coconut milk
1 tablespoon honey
1 teaspoon vanilla extract
5 drops vanilla crème stevia
Pinch of sea salt

Place the can of coconut milk in the refrigerator at least 24 hours before making the whipped cream, so it is well chilled. Chill a metal bowl in the freezer for 15 minutes.

Take the coconut milk out of the refrigerator and remove the lid. Gently scoop out the coconut fat, placing it in the chilled bowl. Pour the remaining liquid into a glass jar and store in the refrigerator, saving it for another use.

Using a handheld blender, whip the coconut milk fat until light and fluffy, about 1 minute. Whip in the honey, vanilla extract, stevia, and salt.

Use right away or store in a glass jar in the refrigerator for up to 24 hours.

Strawberry Applesauce

SERVES 6 ⊙ SWEETNESS: MEDIUM ⊙ Ⓜ Ⓥ

Each fall, when the tree in our backyard is heavy with fruit, the boys and I have a wonderful time harvesting apples, then peeling, coring, and chopping them to prepare applesauce. On special occasions I serve this as a side dish with dinner.

6 medium apples, peeled, cored, and chopped

2 cups fresh strawberries, hulled and halved

¾ cup apple juice

1 tablespoon freshly squeezed lemon juice

1 tablespoon vanilla extract

1 teaspoon ground cinnamon

Preheat the oven to 350°F.

Toss together the apples, strawberries, apple juice, lemon juice, vanilla extract, and cinnamon in a 2-quart baking dish with a lid.

Bake, covered, for 60 to 90 minutes, until the apples are soft. Let the apples cool for 1 hour, then mash with a potato masher and serve.

Pies, Pastries, and Crusts

Coconut Cream Tart ◉ 96

Coconut Macadamia Tart Crust ◉ 97

Peach Cherry Crisp ◉ 98

Strawberry Rhubarb Crisp with
 Coconut Topping ◉ 99

Upside-Down Apple Tartlets ◉ 101

Shallot Tart Crust ◉ 102

Coconut Cream Tart

SERVES 12 ● SWEETNESS: LOW ● **Ⓥ**

I've been making raw coconut cream pies for years. Cracking the coconuts and scooping out the meat makes this a very laborious dish, but Katie, who blogs about desserts on *Chocolate-Covered Katie*, introduced me to the idea of using zucchini in the filling, which reduces the amount of coconut needed and hence the amount of labor necessary. Another plus? You get a healthy vegetable in your creamy mousse-like dessert. To crack a coconut, turn it on its side. Using a sharp, heavy cleaver, chop off the top point of the coconut. You will be left with the white flesh on top. Puncture the flesh with the knife and pour the coconut water into a cup. Turn the coconut back on its side and chop it in half. Once open, use a spoon to scoop out the white coconut meat.

1^1/$_2$ cups fresh young coconut meat, from 2 to 3 coconuts

1 small zucchini, peeled and chopped (about 1 cup)

^{3}/$_4$ cup coconut oil, at room temperature

^{1}/$_4$ cup fresh coconut water

^{1}/$_4$ cup coconut sugar

1 teaspoon vanilla extract

^{1}/$_8$ teaspoon vanilla crème stevia

^{1}/$_8$ teaspoon sea salt

1 Coconut Macadamia Tart Crust (opposite)

In a high-powered blender, puree the coconut meat, zucchini, coconut oil, coconut water, and coconut sugar until very smooth. Blend in the vanilla extract, stevia, and salt until thoroughly combined. Pour the mixture into the piecrust.

Refrigerate until the pie has set, about 3 hours, then serve.

Coconut Macadamia Tart Crust

MAKES ONE 9-INCH CRUST ⊙ Ⓥ

Use this raw crust as a delightfully rich, crunchy base for the Coconut Cream Tart (opposite), or fill it with a chocolate concoction of your own devising.

1 cup macadamia nuts

1 cup unsweetened shredded coconut

¹/₈ teaspoon sea salt

1 tablespoon coconut oil, at room temperature

1 teaspoon water

In a food processor, pulse together the macadamia nuts, shredded coconut, and salt. Add the coconut oil and water and process until the dough forms a ball. Press the dough evenly into the bottom and up the sides of a 9-inch metal tart pan with a removable bottom.

Refrigerate for 30 minutes before filling.

Peach Cherry Crisp

SERVES 6 ⦿ SWEETNESS: MEDIUM

Naturally sweet peaches and cherries come together to create an incredibly perfumed filling in this nutty, almond-scented crisp.

Filling
2 (10-ounce) bags frozen peaches
1 (10-ounce) bag frozen cherries
1 tablespoon arrowroot powder
1 tablespoon vanilla extract

Topping
1 cup blanched almond flour
¼ teaspoon baking soda
¼ teaspoon sea salt
2 tablespoons coconut oil, at room
   temperature
2 tablespoons honey
1 cup sliced almonds

Preheat the oven to 350°F.

To make the filling, place the peaches, cherries, arrowroot powder, and vanilla extract in a large bowl and toss to combine. Transfer the mixture to a 2-quart round baking dish with a lid.

Bake, covered, for 30 to 40 minutes, until the fruits release some of their liquid and the mixture is slightly thickened.

To make the topping, pulse together the almond flour, baking soda, and salt in a food processor. Add the coconut oil and honey and pulse until a dough forms. Remove the blade from the food processor and work the almonds into the dough with your hands. Sprinkle the topping over the fruit. Cover the dish with the lid.

Bake for an additional 25 to 35 minutes, until the topping is golden brown and the juices are bubbling. Remove the lid and bake uncovered for an additional 5 to 10 minutes. Let the crisp cool for 20 minutes, then serve warm.

Strawberry Rhubarb Crisp with Coconut Topping

SERVES 6 ⊙ SWEETNESS: LOW ⊙ Ⓜ

Tart rhubarb and fresh strawberries are a classic combination, but adding a crispy golden coconut topping makes this lightly sweetened treat an original.

Filling
6 stalks rhubarb, cut into $1/8$-inch slices (about $1^1/2$ cups)
2 pounds fresh strawberries, hulled
2 tablespoons arrowroot powder
$1/4$ cup freshly squeezed orange juice

Topping
1 cup unsweetened shredded coconut
$1/4$ cup golden flax meal
2 tablespoons coconut flour
$1/2$ teaspoon sea salt
$1/4$ cup coconut oil, at room temperature
2 tablespoons honey

Preheat the oven to 350°F.

To make the filling, place the rhubarb and strawberries in a 2-quart baking dish with a lid. In a small bowl, dissolve the arrowroot powder in the orange juice, stirring until thoroughly combined. Add the arrowroot mixture to the fruit, tossing to combine.

To make the topping, pulse together the shredded coconut, flax meal, coconut flour, and salt in a food processor. Add the coconut oil and honey and pulse until a dough forms. Sprinkle the topping over the fruit. Cover the dish with the lid.

Bake for 30 to 40 minutes, until the fruit juices are bubbling. Remove the lid and bake uncovered for an additional 5 to 10 minutes. Let the crisp cool for 15 minutes, then serve warm.

Upside-Down Apple Tartlets

SERVES 8 ⊙ SWEETNESS: MEDIUM ⊙ Ⓥ

Use Honeycrisp or Braeburn apples for this dessert and serve with Coconut Whipped Cream (page 93). My friend Shirley, of the blog *Gluten Free Easily*, taught me to make pie with the crust on top.

Crust
2 cups blanched almond flour
$\frac{1}{2}$ teaspoon sea salt
$\frac{1}{4}$ cup coconut oil, at room temperature
$\frac{1}{4}$ teaspoon vanilla crème stevia

Filling
6 large apples, peeled, cored, and cut into $\frac{1}{4}$-inch slices
1 cup apple juice
1 tablespoon freshly squeezed lemon juice
2 tablespoons arrowroot powder
1 tablespoon ground cinnamon

Preheat the oven to 350°F. Place eight 1-cup wide-mouth Mason jars on a large baking sheet.

To make the crust, pulse together the almond flour and salt in a food processor. Add the coconut oil and stevia and pulse until the mixture forms a ball. Transfer the dough to a piece of parchment paper and place in the freezer for 20 minutes.

To make the filling, place the apples, apple juice, lemon juice, arrowroot powder, and cinnamon in a large bowl, and toss to combine. Transfer the apples to the Mason jars so that each one is overfull. Divide the remaining juice from the bottom of the bowl between the jars.

Remove the dough from the freezer, place between 2 pieces of parchment paper generously dusted with almond flour, and roll out the dough $\frac{1}{4}$ inch thick. Remove the top sheet of parchment. Using the top of a wide-mouth Mason jar, cut out 8 circles of dough and place one on top of each apple-filled Mason jar.

Bake for 40 to 50 minutes, until the juices are bubbling and the crust is golden brown. Serve the tartlets hot out of the oven.

< Upside-Down Apple Tartlets with Coconut Whipped Cream (page 93)

Shallot Tart Crust

MAKES ONE 9-INCH CRUST

Pair this deliciously simple crust with my Bacon Tart (page 79),
or create your own quiche-like filling using green vegetables and
eggs. See photo on page 78.

1¼ cups blanched almond flour

½ teaspoon sea salt

1 large egg

¼ cup Spectrum all-vegetable
   shortening

1 shallot, minced (about 1 tablespoon)

Preheat the oven to 350°F.

In a food processor, pulse together
the almond flour and salt. Pulse in the
egg and shortening, then pulse in the
shallots until the dough forms a ball.
Press the dough evenly into the bottom
and up the sides of a 9-inch metal tart
pan with a removable bottom.

Bake for 6 to 8 minutes, until the
crust is golden. Remove from the oven
and let cool completely before filling.

Ice Cream

Coffee Ice Cream ◉ 104

Mint Chip Ice Cream ◉ 105

"Peanut Butter" Ice Cream ◉ 106

Chocolate Sorbet ◉ 108

Cookie Dough Ice Cream ◉ 109

Key Lime Ice Cream ◉ 110

Coffee Ice Cream

SERVES 4 ● SWEETNESS: MEDIUM ● Ⓜ

A rich, creamy base infused with the alluring flavor of roasted coffee appeals to both adults and children. My friend Kelly at the Spunky Coconut website wrote my favorite ice cream book of all time. This recipe is an adaptation of one from her book *The Spunky Coconut Dairy-Free Ice Cream.*

¹/₃ cup organic decaf coffee beans, very finely ground

1 cup boiling water

¹/₃ cup hemp seeds

1 (13-ounce) can coconut milk

2 tablespoons coconut oil, at room temperature

¹/₃ cup honey

¹/₄ teaspoon vanilla crème stevia

Place the ground coffee in a Mason jar and add the boiling water. Let steep for 15 minutes, then strain the coffee into a clean Mason jar; discard the coffee grounds. Place the jar of coffee in the freezer for 10 minutes to cool.

In a high-powered blender, puree the hemp seeds and coffee until very smooth. Blend in the coconut milk, coconut oil, honey, and stevia until thoroughly combined.

Pour the mixture into an ice cream maker and freeze, following the manufacturer's instructions. Serve immediately.

Let any leftover ice cream melt and store in the refrigerator for up to 2 days before refreezing in an ice cream maker.

Mint Chip Ice Cream

SERVES 4 ◉ SWEETNESS: MEDIUM ◉ Ⓝ

In my never-ending quest to reduce the amount of sugar that
I consume, I created this minty ice cream speckled with dark
chocolate—it uses a little more stevia and a little less honey than
my other recipes.

1 (13-ounce) can coconut milk
$1/3$ cup hemp seeds
$1/3$ cup water
$1/4$ cup honey
$1^1/2$ teaspoons peppermint extract
$1/4$ teaspoon vanilla crème stevia
$1/4$ cup dark chocolate chips

In a high-powered blender, puree the coconut milk, hemp seeds, and water until very smooth. Blend in the honey, peppermint extract, and stevia, then add the chocolate chips, blending just until broken into very small pieces.

Pour the mixture into an ice cream maker and freeze, following the manufacturer's instructions. Serve immediately.

Let any leftover ice cream melt and store in the refrigerator for up to 2 days before refreezing in an ice cream maker.

"Peanut Butter" Ice Cream

SERVES 4 ⊙ SWEETNESS: MEDIUM ⊙ Ⓜ

I use sunflower seed butter in this recipe since I don't eat peanuts (a mold-ridden and highly allergenic legume). I love its intense, nutty flavor, and I don't miss the peanuts a bit. With a few naturally rich ingredients, it doesn't take sugar and cream to make this ice cream sing.

1 (13-ounce) can coconut milk
1 tablespoon coconut oil, at room temperature
1/4 cup honey
1/4 cup sunflower seed butter
1/4 teaspoon vanilla crème stevia
1/8 teaspoon sea salt

In a high-powered blender, puree the coconut milk and coconut oil until very smooth. Blend in the honey, sunflower seed butter, stevia, and salt until thoroughly combined.

Pour the mixture into an ice cream maker and freeze, following the manufacturer's instructions. Serve immediately.

Let any leftover ice cream melt and store in the refrigerator for up to 2 days before refreezing in an ice cream maker.

Chocolate Sorbet (page 108), >
Cookie Dough Ice Cream (page 109),
and "Peanut Butter" Ice Cream

Chocolate Sorbet

SERVES 4 ● SWEETNESS: MEDIUM ● Ⓜ

Made from rich dark chocolate and a bit of sweetener, dairy-free sorbet never tasted so rich and creamy. It's decadence in a spoon. See photo on page 107.

¹/₄ cup honey
2 cups water
1 cup dark chocolate chips
¹/₈ teaspoon vanilla crème stevia

In a saucepan over medium heat, dissolve the honey in the water. Remove from the heat and stir in the chocolate chips and stevia until completely melted. Transfer the mixture to a high-powered blender and puree until smooth.

Pour the mixture into an ice cream maker and freeze, following the manufacturer's instructions. Serve immediately.

Let any leftover sorbet melt and store in the refrigerator for up to 2 days before refreezing in an ice cream maker.

Cookie Dough Ice Cream

SERVES 4 ● SWEETNESS: HIGH

Making vanilla ice cream without cream is the holy grail for those who make dairy-free ice cream. Although this recipe took many, many tries to perfect, you'll be more than happy with its smooth, creamy vanilla flavor and its crunchy chocolate chips enrobed in cookie dough. See photo on page 107.

1 (13-ounce) can coconut milk

1/4 cup hemp seeds

1/4 cup honey

3 tablespoons coconut oil, at room temperature

2 tablespoons water

1 tablespoon vanilla extract

1/8 teaspoon vanilla crème stevia

1/8 teaspoon sea salt

1 vanilla bean pod

1/2 cup dough from Paleo Chocolate Chip Cookies (page 118)

In a high-powered blender, puree the coconut milk, hemp seeds, honey, coconut oil, and water until very smooth. Blend in the vanilla extract, stevia, and salt until thoroughly combined. Split the vanilla bean pod lengthwise and scrape the seeds into the blender. Blend briefly to combine.

Pour the mixture into an ice cream maker and freeze, following the manufacturer's instructions. When the ice cream is almost ready, drop small chunks of the cookie dough into the ice cream maker, then finish processing. Serve immediately.

Let any leftover ice cream melt and store in the refrigerator for up to 2 days before refreezing in an ice cream maker.

Key Lime Ice Cream

SERVES 4 ◉ SWEETNESS: MEDIUM ◉ Ⓜ

My boys love it when I make Key lime pie, and this Key Lime Ice Cream is one of their favorites. Add a tablespoon of fresh lime zest to enhance the citrus flavor and add beautiful flecks of green to the ice cream.

1 (13-ounce) can coconut milk

2 tablespoons hemp seeds

1/2 cup freshly squeezed lime juice

1/4 cup honey

2 tablespoons coconut oil, at room temperature

1/4 teaspoon vanilla crème stevia

In a high-powered blender, puree the coconut milk and hemp seeds until very smooth. Blend in the lime juice, honey, coconut oil, and stevia until thoroughly combined.

Pour the mixture into an ice cream maker and freeze, following the manufacturer's instructions. Serve immediately.

Let any leftover ice cream melt and store in the refrigerator for up to 2 days before refreezing in an ice cream maker.

Cookies and Bars

Chocolate Mint Cookies ◉ 112

Cinnamon Raisin Cookies ◉ 113

Coconut Crunch Bars ◉ 114

Lime Bars ◉ 115

Flourless Nut-Free Brownies ◉ 117

Paleo Chocolate Chip Cookies ◉ 118

Chocolate Mint Cookies

MAKES 24 COOKIES ● SWEETNESS: HIGH

Serve this minty double chocolate chip cookie at your gluten-free holiday cookie exchange with warming Spicy Chai (page 120). Alternatively, use these to make mint-flavored ice cream sandwiches.

2^1/$_4$ cups blanched almond flour

^{1}/$_4$ cup unsweetened cocoa powder

^{1}/$_2$ teaspoon baking soda

^{1}/$_4$ teaspoon sea salt

^{1}/$_2$ cup Spectrum all-vegetable shortening

^{1}/$_3$ cup honey

1 teaspoon peppermint extract

^{3}/$_4$ cup dark chocolate chips

Preheat the oven to 350°F. Line 2 large baking sheets with parchment paper.

In a food processor, pulse together the almond flour, cocoa powder, baking soda, and salt. Add the shortening, honey, and peppermint extract and pulse until the dough forms a ball. Remove the blade from the food processor and stir in the chocolate chips. Scoop the dough 1 tablespoon at a time onto the prepared baking sheets, pressing down with your palm to flatten, leaving 2 inches between each cookie.

Bake for 5 to 7 minutes, until the tops of the cookies look dry and start to crack. Let the cookies cool on the baking sheets for 20 minutes, then serve warm.

Cinnamon Raisin Cookies

MAKES 14 COOKIES ⊙ SWEETNESS: MEDIUM

Sometimes I miss big, hearty oatmeal cookies. With their plump raisins, spicy cinnamon, and nutty flax meal, you'd never guess that these moist yet crunchy cookies are grain-free.

$^3/_4$ cup blanched almond flour

$^3/_4$ cup golden flax meal

1 tablespoon ground cinnamon

$^1/_2$ teaspoon ground allspice

$^1/_2$ teaspoon sea salt

$^1/_4$ teaspoon baking soda

$^1/_3$ cup Spectrum all-vegetable shortening

$^1/_4$ cup honey

$^1/_4$ cup raisins

Preheat the oven to 350°F. Line 2 large baking sheets with parchment paper.

In a food processor, pulse together the almond flour, flax meal, cinnamon, allspice, salt, and baking soda. Add the shortening and honey and pulse until the dough forms a ball. Remove the blade from the food processor and stir in the raisins. Scoop the dough 1 tablespoon at a time onto the prepared baking sheets, pressing down with your palm to flatten, leaving 2 inches between each cookie.

Bake for 7 to 10 minutes, until golden brown. Let the cookies cool on the baking sheets for 20 minutes, then serve warm.

Coconut Crunch Bars

MAKES 32 BARS ⦿ SWEETNESS: MEDIUM ⦿ Ⓥ

These satisfyingly sweet treats make a great breakfast in a pinch
or the perfect after-school snack. Given how rich these bars are,
a small serving goes quite a long way.

1¹/₂ cups macadamia nuts

¹/₄ cup golden flax meal

¹/₄ cup unsweetened shredded coconut

¹/₄ teaspoon sea salt

¹/₂ cup coconut oil, at room temperature

¹/₂ cup Medjool dates, pitted and chopped

¹/₄ cup macadamia nut butter

In a food processor, pulse together the macadamia nuts, flax meal, shredded coconut, and salt until the mixture is the texture of coarse gravel. Add the coconut oil, dates, and macadamia nut butter and pulse until thoroughly combined. Press the mixture into an 8-inch square baking dish.

Chill in the refrigerator for about 1 hour, or until the mixture is set.

Remove from the refrigerator, cut into 16 squares, then cut each square on the diagonal to make a triangle, and serve.

Store covered in the refrigerator for up to 3 days.

Lime Bars

MAKES 12 BARS ● SWEETNESS: HIGH

A bit of sunshine any time of year, refreshing lime bars are a classic treat for those rare guests who frown upon chocolate indulgences.

Crust
1$^1/_2$ cups blanched almond flour
$^1/_4$ teaspoon sea salt
2 tablespoons coconut oil, melted over very low heat
$^1/_8$ teaspoon vanilla crème stevia

Topping
$^1/_2$ cup freshly squeezed lime juice
3 large eggs
$^1/_4$ cup coconut oil, at room temperature
$^1/_4$ cup honey

Preheat the oven to 350°F. Grease an 8-inch square baking dish with coconut oil and dust with almond flour.

To make the crust, combine the almond flour and salt in a food processor. Pulse in the coconut oil and stevia until thoroughly combined. Press the dough into the bottom of the prepared baking dish.

Bake the crust for 12 to 17 minutes, until golden.

While the crust bakes, prepare the topping. In a high-powered blender, puree the lime juice, eggs, coconut oil, and honey until smooth.

When the crust is ready, remove it from the oven. Pour the topping over the hot crust.

Return to the oven and bake for 18 to 22 minutes, until the topping is golden. Let the bars cool in the baking dish for 30 minutes, then refrigerate for 2 hours to set. Cut into 12 squares and serve.

Store covered in the refrigerator for up to 2 days.

Flourless Nut-Free Brownies

MAKES 16 BROWNIES ◉ SWEETNESS: HIGH ◉ Ⓜ

At last! A rich, melt-in-your-mouth, gluten-free, dairy-free, nut-free brownie. Serve with a scoop of "Peanut Butter" Ice Cream (page 106) for an over-the-top treat.

1 cup dark chocolate chips
$1/4$ cup Spectrum all-vegetable shortening
1 cup coconut sugar
4 large eggs
1 tablespoon vanilla extract

Preheat the oven to 350°F. Grease an 8-inch square baking dish with shortening.

In a medium saucepan over very low heat, melt the chocolate chips until smooth. Remove the pan from the heat, then mix in the shortening and coconut sugar. Stir in the eggs and vanilla extract until thoroughly combined. Pour the batter into the prepared baking dish.

Bake for 20 to 25 minutes, until a toothpick inserted into the center of the brownies comes out with just a few moist crumbs attached.

Let the brownies cool in the baking dish for 1 hour. Cut into 16 squares and serve.

Paleo Chocolate Chip Cookies

MAKES 24 COOKIES ◉ SWEETNESS: MEDIUM

You'll need a food processor to blend all of the ingredients for this recipe—it won't work if you make it by hand—but the result is the perfect Paleo cookie. For summertime fun, fill these with the vanilla base from my Cookie Dough Ice Cream (page 109) to make ice cream sandwiches.

2 cups blanched almond flour

$1/2$ teaspoon baking soda

$1/4$ teaspoon sea salt

$1/4$ cup Spectrum all-vegetable shortening

$1/4$ cup honey

1 tablespoon vanilla extract

$1/2$ cup dark chocolate chips

Preheat the oven to 350°F. Line 2 large baking sheets with parchment paper.

In a food processor, pulse together the almond flour, baking soda, and salt. Add the shortening, honey, and vanilla extract and pulse until thoroughly combined. Remove the blade from the food processor and stir in the chocolate chips. Scoop the dough 1 tablespoon at a time onto the prepared baking sheets, pressing down with your palm to flatten, leaving 2 inches between each cookie.

Bake for 6 to 9 minutes, until golden brown. Let the cookies cool on the baking sheets for 20 minutes, then serve warm.

Beverages

Spicy Chai ☉ 120

Dandelion Root Coffee ☉ 121

Flax Meal Tea ☉ 122

Ginger Ale ☉ 123

Mojito Mocktail ☉ 124

Strawberry Basil Soda ☉ 126

Almond Milk ☉ 127

Spicy Chai

SERVES 4 ⊙ Ⓜ Ⓥ

The word *chai* simply means "tea," and many families have their own special formula that has been passed down from one generation to the next. Chintzy store-bought chai tea bags, which contain a mixture of ground spices, lose their freshness quickly, so I make my own aromatic chai with beautiful whole spices. If you like, serve this drink with coconut milk and stevia.

6 cups water

3 tablespoons peeled and minced fresh ginger

3 cinnamon sticks

3 cardamom pods

3 cloves

3 peppercorns

1 tablespoon loose peppermint tea

In a saucepan over medium heat, bring the water and ginger to a boil. Lower the heat, add the cinnamon, cardamom, cloves, peppercorns, and peppermint tea, and simmer for 10 minutes.

Pour the chai through a fine-mesh strainer into 4 mugs and serve.

Dandelion Root Coffee

SERVES 4 ⊙ Ⓜ Ⓥ

Deliciously bitter dandelion root coffee is a wonderful caffeine-free substitute for traditional coffee and a great liver cleanser as well. I purchase my roasted dandelion root and roasted chicory root online from Starwest Botanicals at Amazon.com, as it can be challenging to find in retail stores. If the roots you purchase aren't already finely ground, use a coffee grinder.

6 cups water
2 tablespoons finely ground roasted dandelion root
2 tablespoons finely ground roasted chicory
2 cinnamon sticks

In a saucepan over medium heat, combine the water, dandelion root, chicory, and cinnamon sticks and bring to a boil. Lower the heat and simmer for 10 minutes.

Pour the mixture though a fine-mesh strainer to remove the grounds, then serve.

Flax Meal Tea

SERVES 1 ○ Ⓜ Ⓥ

Flax is rich in omega-3 fatty acids and full of good fiber. Incidentally, I found in a test group of one (I love being my own guinea pig) that drinking this soothing beverage every day for 7 weeks lowered my total cholesterol by 30 points. I also find it supports good digestion.

1 tablespoon brown flax meal
1¹/₂ cups boiling water

Place the flax meal in a large mug, then fill with the boiling water.

Let stand for 10 minutes to thicken, then serve.

Ginger Ale

SERVES 4 ⊙ Ⓜ Ⓥ

Ginger is an anti-inflammatory, and it has antibacterial and antiviral properties as well. While a tickle in the throat during the cold of winter calls for a hearty dose of Spicy Chai (page 120), summertime ailments are better served with the piquant bite of ginger in this sweet and refreshing drink.

2 cups ice cubes

3 tablespoons peeled and minced fresh ginger

$1/4$ teaspoon stevia

1 cup water

1 quart sparkling water

Lemon wedges, for garnish

Prepare 4 glasses by placing $1/2$ cup of the ice in each. Set aside.

In a high-powered blender, puree the ginger, stevia, and water until smooth. Pour the mixture through a fine-mesh strainer to remove the pulp. Pour $1/4$ cup of the ginger mixture into each glass. Fill the remainder of each glass with sparkling water and stir. Garnish each glass with a lemon wedge and serve.

Mojito Mocktail

SERVES 4 ⊙ Ⓜ Ⓥ

Although I no longer drink alcohol because of its lack of nutrients, I love a fancy cocktail as much as the next girl. Here's a healthy twist on one of my favorites. For a festive touch, top this tart drink with an emerald-colored slice of lime and a sprig of mint.

2 cups ice cubes

$1/2$ cup coarsely chopped fresh mint leaves

3 limes, peeled

$1/8$ teaspoon stevia

1 cup water

1 quart sparkling water

Lime slices, for garnish

Mint sprigs, for garnish

Prepare 4 glasses by placing $1/2$ cup of the ice in each. Set aside.

In a high-powered blender, puree the mint, limes, stevia, and water until smooth. Pour the mixture through a fine-mesh strainer to remove the pulp. Pour $1/4$ cup of the mojito mixture into each glass. Fill the remainder of each glass with sparkling water and stir. Garnish each glass with a slice of lime and a sprig of mint and serve.

Strawberry Basil Soda

SERVES 4 ◦ Ⓜ Ⓥ

You may have tasted the wonderful combination of strawberries and basil in a salad, and now you can drink it too! While my children enjoy fun, festive beverages, little do they know that the ones I serve them are packed with super-healthy micronutrients. Make this summery drink to put a dent in a big basil harvest.

2 cups ice cubes
1 cup fresh strawberries, hulled and
  halved, plus more for garnish
$1/2$ cup coarsely chopped fresh basil
$1/4$ teaspoon stevia
1 cup water
1 quart sparkling water

Prepare 4 glasses by placing $1/2$ cup of the ice in each. Set aside.

In a high-powered blender, puree the strawberries, basil, stevia, and water until smooth. Pour the mixture through a fine-mesh strainer to remove the pulp. Pour $1/4$ cup of the strawberry mixture into each glass. Fill the remainder of each glass with sparkling water and stir. Garnish each glass with a strawberry and serve.

Almond Milk

Naturally sweet and creamy, almond milk is a great alternative to cow's milk. I like it on Super Spice Granola (page 29) and in Dandelion Root Coffee (page 121).

2 cups raw almonds
1 vanilla bean
4 cups water

Fill a large bowl with water and soak the almonds and vanilla bean overnight.

In a fine-mesh strainer, drain and thoroughly rinse the almonds and vanilla bean. Discard the soaking water. In a high-powered blender, puree the almonds, vanilla bean, and the 4 cups of water until smooth.

Strain the mixture through a piece of cheesecloth, discarding the solids.

Store in a glass jar in the refrigerator for up to 2 days.

Sources

Almond Flour

Honeyville
888-810-3212
www.honeyvillegrain.com

Lucy's Kitchen Shop
888-484-2126
www.lucyskitchenshop.com

Nuts.com
800-558-6887
www.nutsonline.com

Arrowroot Powder

More Than Alive
800-516-5911
www.morethanalive.com

Chocolate

Dagoba Chocolate
866-972-6879
www.dagobachocolate.com

Kallari Chocolate
877-992-4626
www.chocosphere.com

Coconut Butter and Coconut Cream Concentrate

Artisana
866-237-8688
www.artisanafoods.com

Tropical Traditions
866-311-2626
www.tropicaltraditions.com

Coconut Flour

Nuts.com
800-558-6887
www.nutsonline.com

Coconut Milk

Thai Kitchen
800-967-8424
www.thaikitchen.com

Coconut Oil

Spectrum
866-595-8917
www.spectrumorganics.com

Coconut Palm Sugar

Sweet Tree
541-488-5605
www.bigtreefarms.com

Egg White Protein Powder

Frank Zane
800-323-7537
www.frankzane.com

Food Processor

Cuisinart 14-cup food processor
800-726-0190
www.cuisinart.com

High-Powered Blender

Vitamix
800-848-2649
www.vitamix.com

Honey

Madhava
800-530-2900
www.madhavasweeteners.com

Loaf Pan

Magic Line
866-716-2433
www.cheftools.com

Salt

Selina Naturally
800-867-7258
www.celticseasalt.com

Sesame Oil

Eden
888-424-3336
www.edenfoods.com

Shortening

Spectrum
866-595-8917
www.spectrumorganics.com

Spice Blends

Spice Hunter
800-444-3061
www.spicehunter.com

Stevia

SweetLeaf
800-899-9908
www.sweetleaf.com

Ume Plum Vinegar

Eden
888-424-3336
www.edenfoods.com

Vanilla Extract

Flavorganics
866-972-6879
www.flavorganics.com

Index

A

Allergies, 2
Almond butter, 14
    Sesame Noodles, 58
    Tangy "Peanut"
        Sauce, 90
Almond flour, 10, 128
    Bagels, 19
    Banana Bread, 40
    Blueberry Coffee
        Cake, 24
    Chocolate Mint
        Cookies, 112
    Cinnamon Raisin
        Cookies, 113
    Garlic Crackers, 43
    Lime Bars, 115
    Olive Oil Thyme
        Crackers, 44
    Paleo Bread, 34
    Paleo Chocolate Chip
        Cookies, 118
    Paleo Pancakes, 22
    Peach Cherry
        Crisp, 98
    Rye Bread, 37
    Sesame Fish Sticks, 72
    Shallot Tart
        Crust, 102
    Upside-Down Apple
        Tartlets, 101

Almonds
    Almond Milk, 127
    Peach Cherry Crisp, 98
    Rice Pilaf, 51
Apples
    Chicken Salad, 67
    Cran-Apple Power
        Bars, 27
    Strawberry
        Applesauce, 94
    Upside-Down Apple
        Tartlets, 101
Apricot Muffins, 20
Arrowroot powder, 10, 128
Asian Stir-Fry, 82
Autoimmune conditions,
    2, 4
Avocado
    Avocado Kale Salad, 46
Ayurveda, 1–2

B

Bacon Tart, 79
Bagels, 19
Balsamic Rosemary
    Beets, 53
Banana Bread, 40
Bars. See Cookies and bars
Basil
    Basil Cream Sauce, 86
    Strawberry Basil
        Soda, 126
    Vegan Pesto Rustico, 90

Beans, 7
Beef
    Beef with Broccoli, 84
    Marinated Flank
        Steak, 81
    Paleo Shepherd's Pie, 71
    Stuffed Mushrooms, 57
Beets, Balsamic
    Rosemary, 53
Beta-carotene, 62
Beverages
    Almond Milk, 127
    Dandelion Root
        Coffee, 121
    Flax Meal Tea, 122
    Ginger Ale, 123
    Mojito Mocktail, 124
    Spicy Chai, 120
    Strawberry Basil
        Soda, 126
    Strawberry Power Piña
        Colada, 32
Bitter Dandelion Greens, 47
Blenders, high-powered,
    16, 129
Blueberries
    Blueberry Coffee
        Cake, 24
    Cherry Berry Syrup, 92
Bok choy
    Asian Stir-Fry, 82
    Pad Thai, 61

Bread
  Banana Bread, 40
  Cinnamon French
    Toast, 26
  Date Orange Bread, 39
  Nut-Free Bread, 36
  Paleo Bread, 34
  Paleo Tortillas, 41
  Rye Bread, 37
Breakfast
  Apricot Muffins, 20
  Bagels, 19
  Blueberry Coffee
    Cake, 24
  Breakfast Sausage, 31
  Cinnamon French
    Toast, 26
  Cran-Apple Power
    Bars, 27
  Crepes, 23
  Hot Cereal, 28
  Nut-Free Bran
    Muffins, 21
  Paleo Pancakes, 22
  Strawberry Power Piña
    Colada, 32
  Super Spice
    Granola, 29
Broccoli
  Asian Stir-Fry, 82
  Beef with Broccoli, 84
  Green Frittata, 80
  Pad Thai, 61
  Roasted Broccoli, 56
Brownies, Flourless
    Nut-Free, 117
Burdock root
  Healing Vegetable
    Bisque, 55
Burgers
  Classic Salmon
    Burgers, 76
  Greek Turkey
    Burgers, 77

C
Cabbage
  Colorful Winter
    Salad, 48
  Mushroom Lo Mein, 60
  Primal Coleslaw, 46
Caesar Dressing, 87
Cake, Blueberry Coffee, 24
Carbohydrates, 5
Carrots
  Asian Stir-Fry, 82
  Chicken Gumbo, 66
  Colorful Winter
    Salad, 48
  Healing Vegetable
    Bisque, 55
  Paleo Shepherd's Pie, 71
  Primal Coleslaw, 46
Cashews
  Pad Thai, 61
Cauliflower
  Cauliflower Rice, 50
  Paleo "Potato" Leek
    Soup, 54
  Paleo Shepherd's Pie, 71
  Rice Pilaf, 51
Cereal, Hot, 28
Chai, Spicy, 120
Cherries
  Cherry Berry Syrup, 92
  Peach Cherry Crisp, 98
Chia seeds, 10
  Hot Cereal, 28
Chicken
  Asian Stir-Fry, 82
  Chicken Gumbo, 66
  Chicken Marbella, 68
  Chicken Salad, 67
  Honey Lemon
    Chicken, 65
  Rosemary Lemon
    Chicken, 70
Chocolate, 10, 128
  Chocolate Mint
    Cookies, 112

Chocolate Sorbet, 108
Flourless Nut-Free
    Brownies, 117
Mint Chip Ice
    Cream, 105
Paleo Chocolate Chip
    Cookies, 118
Cinnamon
  Cinnamon French
    Toast, 26
  Cinnamon Raisin
    Cookies, 113
Classic Salmon
    Burgers, 76
Coconut
  Coconut Cream
    Tart, 96
  Coconut Crunch
    Bars, 114
  Coconut Macadamia Tart
    Crust, 97
  Hot Cereal, 28
  Strawberry Rhubarb
    Crisp with Coconut
    Topping, 99
Coconut butter, 10, 128
Coconut cream concentrate,
    10, 128
Coconut flour, 11, 128
  Apricot Muffins, 20
  Banana Bread, 40
  Crepes, 23
  Date Orange Bread, 39
  Nut-Free Bran
    Muffins, 21
  Nut-Free Bread, 36
  Nut-Free Crackers, 42
  Paleo Bread, 34
  Paleo Pancakes, 22
  Paleo Tortillas, 41
  Sesame Fish Sticks, 72
  Strawberry Rhubarb
    Crisp with Coconut
    Topping, 99

Coconut milk, 11, 128
    Basil Cream Sauce, 86
    Cinnamon French
        Toast, 26
    Coconut Whipped
        Cream, 93
    Coffee Ice Cream, 104
    Cookie Dough Ice
        Cream, 109
    Key Lime Ice Cream, 110
    Mint Chip Ice Cream, 105
    "Peanut Butter" Ice
        Cream, 106
    Strawberry Power Piña
        Colada, 32
    Tangy "Peanut" Sauce, 90
Coconut oil, 6, 12, 128
Coconut palm sugar, 12, 129
Cod
    Sesame Fish Sticks, 72
Coffee
    Coffee Ice Cream, 104
    Dandelion Root
        Coffee, 121
Coffee Cake, Blueberry, 24
Coleslaw, Primal, 46
Colorful Winter Salad, 48
Cookies and bars
    Chocolate Mint
        Cookies, 112
    Cinnamon Raisin
        Cookies, 113
    Coconut Crunch
        Bars, 114
    Cookie Dough Ice
        Cream, 109
    Cran-Apple Power
        Bars, 27
    Flourless Nut-Free
        Brownies, 117
    Lime Bars, 115
    Paleo Chocolate Chip
        Cookies, 118
Cordain, Loren, 3, 6, 7

Crackers
    Garlic Crackers, 43
    Nut-Free Crackers, 42
    Olive Oil Thyme
        Crackers, 44
Cran-Apple Power Bars, 27
Crepes, 23
Crisps
    Peach Cherry Crisp, 98
    Strawberry Rhubarb
        Crisp with Coconut
        Topping, 99
Crusts
    Coconut Macadamia Tart
        Crust, 97
    Shallot Tart Crust, 102
Currants
    Rice Pilaf, 51

D

Daikon root
    Healing Vegetable
        Bisque, 55
Dairy products, 7
Dandelion
    Bitter Dandelion
        Greens, 47
    Dandelion Root
        Coffee, 121
Dates
    Coconut Crunch
        Bars, 114
    Date Orange Bread, 39
    Nut-Free Bran
        Muffins, 21
Desserts
    Chocolate Mint
        Cookies, 112
    Chocolate Sorbet, 108
    Cinnamon Raisin
        Cookies, 113
    Coconut Cream Tart, 96
    Coconut Crunch
        Bars, 114
    Coffee Ice Cream, 104

    Cookie Dough Ice
        Cream, 109
    Flourless Nut-Free
        Brownies, 117
    Key Lime Ice Cream, 110
    Lime Bars, 115
    Mint Chip Ice Cream, 105
    Paleo Chocolate Chip
        Cookies, 118
    Peach Cherry Crisp, 98
    "Peanut Butter" Ice
        Cream, 106
    Strawberry Rhubarb
        Crisp with Coconut
        Topping, 99
    Upside-Down Apple
        Tartlets, 101
Dill Tartar Sauce, 88

E

Eaton, S. Boyd, 3
Eggplant, 2
Eggs
    Bacon Tart, 79
    Green Frittata, 80
    guidelines for, 7
Egg white protein powder,
    12, 129
Entrées
    Asian Stir-Fry, 82
    Bacon Tart, 79
    Beef with Broccoli, 84
    Chicken Gumbo, 66
    Chicken Marbella, 68
    Chicken Salad, 67
    Classic Salmon
        Burgers, 76
    Greek Turkey Burgers, 77
    Green Frittata, 80
    Honey Lemon
        Chicken, 65
    Marinated Flank
        Steak, 81
    Mustard Salmon
        Fillet, 75

Paleo Shepherd's Pie, 71
Rosemary Lemon
  Chicken, 70
Salmon Salad, 73
Sesame Fish Sticks, 72

F
Fats, guidelines for, 6
Fiber, 5
Fife, Bruce, 11
Fish
  Classic Salmon
    Burgers, 76
  guidelines for, 5–6
  Mustard Salmon
    Fillet, 75
  Salmon Salad, 73
  Sesame Fish Sticks, 72
Flax meal, 13
  Bagels, 19
  Cinnamon Raisin
    Cookies, 113
  Coconut Crunch
    Bars, 114
  Flax Meal Tea, 122
  Hot Cereal, 28
  Nut-Free Bran
    Muffins, 21
  Nut-Free Bread, 36
  Nut-Free Crackers, 42
  Paleo Bread, 34
  Paleo Pancakes, 22
  Rye Bread, 37
  Strawberry Rhubarb
    Crisp with Coconut
    Topping, 99
Flour. See Almond flour;
  Coconut flour
Flourless Nut-Free
  Brownies, 117
Food allergies, 2
Food processors, 16, 129
French Toast,
  Cinnamon, 26
Frittata, Green, 80

Fruits
  dried, 6
  guidelines for, 6
  juice, 6
  nutritional values of,
    vs. grains, 5
  See also individual fruits

G
Garlic
  Garlic Crackers, 43
  Roasted Garlic, 89
Ginger Ale, 123
Gottschall, Elaine, 2
Grains
  avoiding, 7
  nutritional values of,
    vs. fruits and
    vegetables, 5
Granola, Super Spice, 29
Greek Turkey Burgers, 77
Green Frittata, 80
Gumbo, Chicken, 66

H
Healing Vegetable
  Bisque, 55
Hemp seeds, 13
  Coffee Ice Cream, 104
  Cookie Dough Ice
    Cream, 109
  Key Lime Ice Cream, 110
  Mint Chip Ice Cream, 105
  Nut-Free Crackers, 42
Honey, 13, 129
  Honey Lemon
    Chicken, 65
Hot Cereal, 28

I
Ice cream
  Coffee Ice Cream, 104
  Cookie Dough Ice
    Cream, 109
  Key Lime Ice Cream, 110

  Mint Chip Ice Cream, 105
  "Peanut Butter" Ice
    Cream, 106

K
Kale
  Avocado Kale Salad, 46
  Green Frittata, 80
Kelp noodles
  Mushroom Lo Mein, 60
  Sesame Noodles, 58
Key Lime Ice Cream, 110

L
Leek Soup, Paleo
  "Potato," 54
Legumes, 7
Lemons
  Honey Lemon
    Chicken, 65
  Rosemary Lemon
    Chicken, 70
Lettuce
  Chicken Salad, 67
  Colorful Winter
    Salad, 48
  Salmon Salad, 73
Limes
  Key Lime Ice Cream, 110
  Lime Bars, 115
  Mojito Mocktail, 124
Loaf pans, 16, 129

M
Macadamia nut butter, 14
  Coconut Crunch
    Bars, 114
Macadamia nuts
  Coconut Crunch
    Bars, 114
  Coconut Macadamia Tart
    Crust, 97
  Super Spice Granola, 29
Marinated Flank Steak, 81
Mayonnaise, Paleo, 88

Measurements, 130
Meats, guidelines for, 5. *See also individual meats*
Milk, Almond, 127
Mint
    Chocolate Mint
        Cookies, 112
    Mint Chip Ice Cream, 105
    Mojito Mocktail, 124
Muffins
    Apricot Muffins, 20
    Nut-Free Bran
        Muffins, 21
Mushrooms
    Asian Stir-Fry, 82
    Chicken Gumbo, 66
    Mushroom Lo Mein, 60
    Stuffed Mushrooms, 57
Mustard, 13
    Mustard Salmon
        Fillet, 75
    Very Dijon Salad
        Dressing, 91

N
Nightshade family, 2
Noodles
    Mushroom Lo Mein, 60
    Sesame Noodles, 58
Nut butters, 14. *See also*
    Almond butter;
    Macadamia nut butter
Nut-free recipes
    Apricot Muffins, 20
    Asian Stir-Fry, 82
    Avocado Kale Salad, 46
    Balsamic Rosemary
        Beets, 53
    Basil Cream Sauce, 86
    Beef with Broccoli, 84
    Bitter Dandelion
        Greens, 47
    Breakfast Sausage, 31
    Caesar Dressing, 87
    Cauliflower Rice, 50

Cherry Berry Syrup, 92
Chicken Gumbo, 66
Chicken Marbella, 68
Chicken Salad, 67
Chocolate Sorbet, 108
Classic Salmon
    Burgers, 76
Coconut Whipped
    Cream, 93
Coffee Ice Cream, 104
Colorful Winter Salad, 48
Cookie Dough Ice
    Cream, 109
Crepes, 23
Dandelion Root
    Coffee, 121
Date Orange Bread, 39
Dill Tartar Sauce, 88
Flax Meal Tea, 122
Flourless Nut-Free
    Brownies, 117
Ginger Ale, 123
Greek Turkey Burgers, 77
Green Frittata, 80
Healing Vegetable
    Bisque, 55
Honey Lemon
    Chicken, 65
Key Lime Ice Cream, 110
Marinated Flank
    Steak, 81
Mint Chip Ice Cream, 105
Mojito Mocktail, 124
Mushroom Lo Mein, 60
Mustard Salmon
    Fillet, 75
Nut-Free Bran
    Muffins, 21
Nut-Free Bread, 36
Nut-Free Crackers, 42
Paleo Mayonnaise, 88
Paleo "Potato" Leek
    Soup, 54
Paleo Shepherd's Pie, 71

Paleo Tortillas, 41
"Peanut Butter" Ice
    Cream, 106
Primal Coleslaw, 46
Roasted Broccoli, 56
Roasted Garlic, 89
Rosemary Lemon
    Chicken, 70
Salmon Salad, 73
Salsa Verde, 89
Sautéed Turnips, 56
Spicy Chai, 120
Strawberry
    Applesauce, 94
Strawberry Basil
    Soda, 126
Strawberry Power Piña
    Colada, 32
Stuffed Mushrooms, 57
Tahini Dressing, 91
Twice-Baked Squash, 62
Very Dijon Salad
    Dressing, 91
Nuts
    allergies to, 2
    guidelines for, 6
    See also individual nuts

O
Oils, guidelines for, 6. *See also individual oils*
Olive oil, 6, 14
    Olive Oil Thyme
        Crackers, 44
Olives
    Chicken Marbella, 68
Omega-3 fatty acids, 7, 10, 76, 122
Omega-6 fatty acids, 6, 7
Oranges
    Beef with Broccoli, 84
    Date Orange Bread, 39
    Marinated Flank
        Steak, 81
    Twice-Baked Squash, 62

P

Pad Thai, 61
Paleo Bread, 34
Paleo Chocolate Chip
    Cookies, 118
Paleo diet
    benefits of, 3–4
    exceptions to, 7
    guidelines for, 5–7
    history of, 3
    popularity of, 2
Paleo Mayonnaise, 88
Paleo Pancakes, 22
Paleo "Potato" Leek Soup, 54
Paleo Shepherd's Pie, 71
Paleo Tortillas, 41
Palm oil, 6
Pancakes, Paleo, 22
Peach Cherry Crisp, 98
Peanuts, 6
    "Peanut Butter" Ice
        Cream, 106
    Tangy "Peanut" Sauce, 90
Peppers, 2
Pesto Rustico, Vegan, 90
Pineapple
    Strawberry Power Piña
        Colada, 32
Pine nuts
    Vegan Pesto Rustico, 90
Pork
    Breakfast Sausage, 31
    Stuffed Mushrooms, 57
Potatoes
    avoiding, 2, 6
    Paleo "Potato" Leek
        Soup, 54
Primal Coleslaw, 46
Protein, 5
Prunes
    Chicken Marbella, 68
Pumpkin seeds
    Nut-Free Bran
        Muffins, 21
    Super Spice Granola, 29

R

Raisins
    Cinnamon Raisin
        Cookies, 113
    Nut-Free Bran
        Muffins, 21
    Super Spice Granola, 29
Rhubarb Crisp, Strawberry,
    with Coconut
    Topping, 99
Rice
    Cauliflower Rice, 50
    Rice Pilaf, 51
Roasted Broccoli, 56
Roasted Garlic, 89
Rosemary Lemon
    Chicken, 70
Rye Bread, 37

S

Salad dressings
    Caesar Dressing, 87
    Tahini Dressing, 91
    Very Dijon Salad
        Dressing, 91
Salads
    Avocado Kale Salad, 46
    Chicken Salad, 67
    Colorful Winter Salad, 48
    Primal Coleslaw, 46
    Salmon Salad, 73
Salmon
    Classic Salmon
        Burgers, 76
    Mustard Salmon
        Fillet, 75
    Salmon Salad, 73
    wild vs. farmed, 76
Salsas. See Sauces and
    salsas
Salt, 14, 129
Sauces and salsas
    Basil Cream Sauce, 86
    Dill Tartar Sauce, 88
    Salsa Verde, 89

Strawberry
    Applesauce, 94
    Tangy "Peanut" Sauce, 90
    Vegan Pesto Rustico, 90
Sausage, Breakfast, 31
Sautéed Turnips, 56
Seafood, guidelines for, 5–6.
    See also Fish
Seed butters, 14. See also
    Sunflower seed butter
Seeds, guidelines for, 6. See
    also individual seeds
Sesame oil, 14, 129
    Sesame Noodles, 58
Sesame seeds
    Nut-Free Bran
        Muffins, 21
    Nut-Free Crackers, 42
    Sesame Fish
        Sticks, 72
Shallot Tart Crust, 102
Shepherd's Pie, Paleo, 71
Shortening, 15, 129
Sisson, Mark, 3
Sorbet, Chocolate, 108
Soups
    Healing Vegetable
        Bisque, 55
    Paleo "Potato" Leek
        Soup, 54
Spice blends, 15, 129
Spicy Chai, 120
Squash
    Asian Stir-Fry, 82
    Coconut Cream Tart, 96
    Greek Turkey Burgers, 77
    Pad Thai, 61
    Twice-Baked Squash, 62
Stevia, 15, 129
Stir-Fry, Asian, 82
Strawberries
    Strawberry
        Applesauce, 94
    Strawberry Basil
        Soda, 126

Strawberries, *continued*
 Strawberry Power Piña
  Colada, 32
 Strawberry Rhubarb
  Crisp with Coconut
  Topping, 99
Stuffed Mushrooms, 57
Sunflower seed butter, 14
 "Peanut Butter" Ice
  Cream, 106
Sunflower seeds
 Nut-Free Bran
  Muffins, 21
Super Spice Granola, 29
Syrup, Cherry Berry, 92

T

Tahini Dressing, 91
Tangy "Peanut" Sauce, 90
Tartar Sauce, Dill, 88
Tarts and tartlets
 Bacon Tart, 79
 Coconut Cream Tart, 96
 Coconut Macadamia Tart
  Crust, 97
 Shallot Tart Crust, 102
 Upside-Down Apple
  Tartlets, 101
Tea
 Flax Meal Tea, 122
 Spicy Chai, 120
Tomatoes, 2
Tortillas, Paleo, 41
Turkey
 Breakfast Sausage, 31
 Greek Turkey
  Burgers, 77
Turnips
 Chicken Gumbo, 66
 Sautéed Turnips, 56
Twice-Baked Squash, 62

U

Ume plum vinegar, 15, 129
Upside-Down Apple
 Tartlets, 101

V

Vanilla extract, 16, 129
Vegan recipes
 Almond Milk, 127
 Avocado Kale Salad, 46
 Balsamic Rosemary
  Beets, 53
 Basil Cream Sauce, 86
 Bitter Dandelion
  Greens, 47
 Cauliflower Rice, 50
 Cherry Berry Syrup, 92
 Coconut Cream Tart, 96
 Coconut Crunch
  Bars, 114
 Coconut Macadamia Tart
  Crust, 97
 Colorful Winter Salad, 48
 Dandelion Root
  Coffee, 121
 Flax Meal Tea, 122
 Ginger Ale, 123
 Hot Cereal, 28
 Mojito Mocktail, 124
 Mushroom Lo Mein, 60
 Nut-Free Crackers, 42
 Olive Oil Thyme
  Crackers, 44
 Pad Thai, 61
 Rice Pilaf, 51
 Roasted Broccoli, 56
 Roasted Garlic, 89
 Salsa Verde, 89
 Spicy Chai, 120
 Strawberry
  Applesauce, 94
 Strawberry Basil
  Soda, 126
 Super Spice Granola, 29
 Tahini Dressing, 91
 Tangy "Peanut"
  Sauce, 90
 Upside-Down Apple
  Tartlets, 101
 Vegan Pesto Rustico, 90
 Very Dijon Salad
  Dressing, 91
Vegetables
 guidelines for, 6
 Healing Vegetable
  Bisque, 55
 nutritional values of,
  vs. grains, 5
 See also individual
  vegetables
Very Dijon Salad
 Dressing, 91
Vinegar, ume plum, 15, 129

W

Walnuts
 Cran-Apple Power
  Bars, 27
 Hot Cereal, 28
 Super Spice Granola, 29
 Vegan Pesto Rustico, 90
Whipped Cream,
 Coconut, 93
Wolf, Robb, 3

Z

Zucchini
 Asian Stir-Fry, 82
 Coconut Cream Tart, 96
 Greek Turkey
  Burgers, 77

MEASUREMENT CONVERSION CHARTS

Volume

U.S.	Imperial	Metric
1 tablespoon	$1/2$ fl oz	15 ml
2 tablespoons	1 fl oz	30 ml
$1/4$ cup	2 fl oz	60 ml
$1/3$ cup	3 fl oz	90 ml
$1/2$ cup	4 fl oz	120 ml
$2/3$ cup	5 fl oz ($1/4$ pint)	150 ml
$3/4$ cup	6 fl oz	180 ml
1 cup	8 fl oz ($1/3$ pint)	240 ml
$1^1/4$ cups	10 fl oz ($1/2$ pint)	300 ml
2 cups (1 pint)	16 fl oz ($2/3$ pint)	480 ml
$2^1/2$ cups	20 fl oz (1 pint)	600 ml
1 quart	32 fl oz ($1^2/3$ pints)	1 l

Temperature

Fahrenheit	Celsius/Gas Mark
250°F	120°C/gas mark $1/2$
275°F	135°C/gas mark 1
300°F	150°C/gas mark 2
325°F	160°C/gas mark 3
350°F	180 or 175°C/gas mark 4
375°F	190°C/gas mark 5
400°F	200°C/gas mark 6
425°F	220°C/gas mark 7
450°F	230°C/gas mark 8
475°F	245°C/gas mark 9
500°F	260°C

Length

Inch	Metric
$1/4$ inch	6 mm
$1/2$ inch	1.25 cm
$3/4$ inch	2 cm
1 inch	2.5 cm
6 inches ($1/2$ foot)	15 cm
12 inches (1 foot)	30 cm

Weight

U.S./Imperial	Metric
$1/2$ oz	15 g
1 oz	30 g
2 oz	60 g
$1/4$ lb	115 g
$1/3$ lb	150 g
$1/2$ lb	225 g
$3/4$ lb	350 g
1 lb	450 g

To my Bubby, Molly Amsterdam,
an incredible cook and entrepreneur
who fed me in so many ways.

Copyright © 2013 by Elana Amsterdam
Photographs copyright © 2013 by Leigh Beisch

All rights reserved.
Published in the United States by Ten Speed Press, an imprint of the
Crown Publishing Group, a division of Random House, Inc., New York.
www.crownpublishing.com
www.tenspeed.com

Ten Speed Press and the Ten Speed Press colophon are registered trademarks
of Random House, Inc.

Elana's Pantry™ is a trademark of Elana's Pantry, LLC.
Some of the recipes in this book originally appeared on www.elanaspantry.com.

Library of Congress Cataloging-in-Publication Data is on file with the publisher.

Trade Paperback ISBN: 978-1-60774-551-8
eBook ISBN: 978-1-60774-552-5

Printed in China

Cover design by Betsy Stromberg
Interior design by Chloe Rawlins
Food styling by Dan Becker
Author photo by Francine McDougall

10 9 8 7 6 5 4 3 2 1

First Edition